School Counseling:
New Perspectives & Practices

Edited by
Jackie M. Allen

ERIC/CASS Publications
School of Education
201 Ferguson Building
University of North Carolina at Greensboro
PO Box 26171
Greensboro, NC 27402-6171

ISBN 1-56109-081-6

This publication was funded by the US Department of Education,
Office of Educational Research and Improvement, Contract no.
RR93002004. Opinions expressed in this publication do not
necessarily reflect the positions of the US Department of Education,
OERI, or ERIC/CASS.

Prologue

Gaining access to new ideas and resources is one of the surest ways of improving a current program or practice, or for developing an entirely new approach. This exciting book developed by Jackie Allen offers a wide array of new perspectives and approaches to school counseling. It also offers counseling interventions designed to respond to specific student needs and counseling situations.

Each capsule is prepared as a succinct and cogent analysis of a particular area which can be quickly read. References at the end of each capsule provide additional information and resources. The last chapter, *ERIC/CASS Virtual Libraries: Online Resources for Parents, Teachers, and Counselors*, offers information on the innovative virtual libraries developed by ERIC/CASS which enable counselors to gain access to a variety of online full-text resources.

Special congratulations are due to Jackie Allen for "honcho-ing" this hard-to-"lasso" publication with its exploration of new topics and approaches and the impressive array of producing counselors who *know it like it is*.

We would also like to extend our appreciation to Nancy Perry, Executive Director and Carolyn Sheldon, President, 1997-1998, of the American School Counselor Association for their continuing support and interest in this publication. It has benefited considerably by their support. We are also most appreciative of the thoughtful and interesting introduction provided by Norman Gysbers.

Read, enjoy, and profit from this book and let us know your thoughts and suggestions.

Garry R. Walz
Director

Introduction

School Counseling: New Perspectives and Practices
An Excellent Professional Development Resource

The world in which we live and work is changing and the changes continue to accelerate creating many new challenges. Changing labor markets, a world economy, extended life expectancy, the expectation of lifelong learning, violence in the schools, single-parent families, blended families, cultural and social diversity, substance abuse, and peer and family pressure are some examples of these changes. Herr (1989) provided similar examples when he identified four major societal and individual changes that are having an impact now and will continue to have an impact well into the 21st century. These changes include "the economic climate and the effects of advanced technology, changing family structures, growing pluralism and cultural diversity, and expanded perspectives on populations at risk" (p. 317).

These complex social and economic changes are not abstractions described in our literature and hypothesized to take place sometime in the future. These changes are real and they are occurring now. And, as they occur, they are creating important challenges for society in general but particularly for our schools and the students, parents, and communities they serve.

To respond to these and similar changes occurring in our country, as well as worldwide, requires continued efforts to reform and restructure our schools and the educational programs involved, including guidance. For guidance this means continuing the reforming and restructuring efforts already well underway across the country in which the traditional position orientation of guidance is being enfolded into district-wide K-12 comprehensive guidance programs. For guidance this means becoming an equal partner with other educational programs; not a tacked on ancillary service. For school counselors this means being seen as "program people" who have comprehensive guidance programs to operate in their schools for the benefit of students and parents, in collaboration with teachers and administrators, rather than as "offfce people" who perform mainly school management tasks (Gysbers & Henderson, 1994; 1997).

No guidance programs, no matter how well they are positioned, organized, and operated in the schools however, can guarantee that the students and parents they serve actually receive the benefits of the programs if the school counselors involved have not kept their competence up-to-date because of a lack of involvement in continued professional development. Initial training provides the foundation—the beginning point—to work effectively in the schools. Regular ongoing professional development however, assures continued school counselor competence. For effective professional development to take place school counselors must have access to the best in what is new in professional theory, research, and practices. That is why this book, appropriately titled *School Counseling: New Perspectives and Practices,* is such an important addition to our professional literature.

Within the comprehensive guidance program framework, school counselors are responding everyday to the school-related consequences of many of the complex social and economic changes that are effecting the lives of students and parents. To maintain a high level of competence, to respond appropriately and effectively to the consequences of these changes, school counselors need professional development resources that provide high quality specific and practical information and ideas about best practices. That is what this book is all about.

School Counseling: New Perspectives and Practices brings together in one volume new perspectives and practices drawn from the experiences and expertise of a group of seasoned professionals. These are perspectives and practices that provide practical answers about how to respond to specific problems and issues effecting students and parents. Sample problems and issues that are covered in the book include attention deficit/hyperactivity disorders, at-risk and violence, conflict management, multicultural counseling, and transition counseling.

In addition to providing possible responses to specific problems and issues effecting students and parents, *School Counseling: New Perspectives and Practices* also focuses on possible contextual and system responses school counselors can use to help restructure education and guidance to better serve students and parents. Here a wide range of topics are covered including accountability, credentialling, standards, partnerships, integrated services, school-to-work programs, total quality leadership, and writing and publishing.

In summary, *School Counseling: New Perspectives and Practices* is a rich source of ideas, practices, and techniques to enhance school counselor professional development. The wide range of important topics covered are theoretically sound, but at the same time, the practical ways they are presented, make this book an important source of school counselor professional development. This is a book that is on the "must list" of school counselors' professional development libraries.

Norman C. Gysbers, Ph.D.
Professor
Educational and Counseling
Psychology
University of Missouri-Columbia

References

Gysbers, N.C., & Henderson, P. (1994). *Developing and managing your school guidance program* (2nd ed.). Alexandria, VA: American Counseling Association.

Gysbers, N.C., & Henderson, P. (1997). *Comprehensive guidance programs that work-II* (2nd ed.). Greensboro, NC: ERIC/CASS Publications.

Herr, E.L. (1989). *Counseling in a dynamic society: Opportunities and challenges.* Alexandria, VA: American Association for Counseling and Development.

Preface

The publication of this book is for me, a dream which has become a reality. Several years ago during my presidency of the American School Counselor Association, it became evident that there was a need for articles on practical school counseling topics written by practicing school counselors. Dr. Garry Walz, Director of ERIC Counseling and Student Services Clearinghouse, also sensing the need for a compilation of "hot topics" on school counseling invited me to edit such a series. My intent, in accepting this challenge, was to put together a collection of articles which would speak to the needs of school counselors in their daily practice and provide a resource for counselor education training programs.

In order for the topics to be relevant, the authors must be where the action is in school counseling. Practicing school counselors, national leaders in school counseling, and key counselor educators were invited to write articles. My goal was also to give school counselors, who had not previously written for publication, an opportunity to contribute to the body of knowledge on school counseling. In many cases, I invited the prospective authors to choose the topic about which they would write, motivating them to write with passion about their personal areas of interest and encouraging them to share their expertise with school counselors across the country. The mixture of experienced and new authors, practicing school counselors, and counselor educators added to a diversity of assigned and chosen topics, will offer the reader an excellent combination of expertise and innovations in new perspectives and practices in school counseling.

The "hot topics" in school counseling included in this book are designed to stimulate the reader into thinking in new paradigms, exploring new ideas, inquiring about the possibilities of implementation, and initiating change in their school counseling program. Each author has presented the topic from the perspective of a professional counselor, explaining the importance of the subject for school counselors and making suggestions for the inclusion of this information into the practice of school counseling. Each chapter, therefore, is a place from which to begin, a synopsis of a "hot topic," with excellent references from which to initiate more in-depth reading or research.

The chapters in this monograph fall into three general areas: counseling techniques, program development, and professionalism. The section on counseling techniques emphasizes the diversity of student populations and methods that a school counselor must use to meet individual student needs. Program development focuses on the role of the school counselor in developing a comprehensive developmental school counseling program. The third section on professionalism challenges the school counselor to look beyond the corridors of the local school to the responsibilities and challenges of being a "professional school counselor" in one's community and world.

The "hot topics" on counseling techniques include articles on meeting individual needs, using specialized methods tailored to the particular population. Topics include: student rights, at-risk students and violence, conflict management, learning styles, attention deficit hyperactivity disorder, multicultural counseling, counseling Native students, counseling for high skills, transition counseling, working with parents and teens, and group counseling.

The next group of articles examines the leadership role of the school counselor in education reform. Special skills that school counselors need to improve their programs include: becoming a change agent in education reform, developing a crisis management plan, initiating career development and school-to-work programs, creating a business advisory council, designing an outcome based school counseling system, implementing developmental comprehensive guidance programs, effectively using strategic planning, developing national standards, and initiating home, school and community partnerships.

The concept of the professional school counselor is explored in the last group of articles. The knowledge base of a profession includes more than the skills of the trade; it also includes knowledge and expertise in understanding credentialing and certification, the speciality area of school counseling, the use of technology, and the advanced skills of quality leadership, political astuteness, assessment, advocacy and accountability, and research and publication.

All the authors of the articles in this book have a passion for school counseling. It is a rare privilege to hear from these school counseling leaders. I want to thank each of my school counseling colleagues for their dedication to the profession and for the time and effort they have spent to provide you, the reader, with their unique perspectives about the "hot topics" in the practice of school counseling.

School Counseling: New Perspectives and Practices reveals the depth and breadth of the practice of school counseling. As a profession, school counseling has come of age. The professional school counselor is daily presented with a multitude of challenges from students, parents, administrators, and society. Every school counselor needs a specialized body of knowledge, a mastery of various counseling techniques for diverse student populations, organizational skills for program development and implementation, and the awareness of the significance and importance of school counseling in the local school and in the community and the ability to demonstrate the effectiveness of school counseling programs to the public.

Perhaps you are reading this book to refresh or expand your knowledge on a familiar topic, to learn about some new skills and techniques you can use in your school counseling practice, or maybe to find out what is new in the field. Regardless of your motive, I trust you will gain new ideas and insights from these counseling experts who believe in the contribution that school counseling programs make to the educational system and the importance of school counseling in the lives of youth and their families.

This book is dedicated to the risk takers, the changers, the innovators, the reform agents in education. Consider new paradigms to improve your counseling program, acquire new skills, think and change the status quo. My dream is that you will take these new perspectives and turn them into the reality of innovative school counseling practices now and in the 21st century.

Jackie M. Allen
Spring, 1998

Contents

Counseling Interventions Technologies and Methods

Student Rights

Canary C. Hogan

Overview

Student rights have become the focus of the turmoil that exists in many schools today. With the increasing number of incidences pertaining to violence, and the lawsuits that have challenged procedural operations within schools, teachers and administrators have become more aware of the legal rights of students and of themselves as educators.

The struggle for power and equality by students continues to take place in schools and in the courts. Students are challenging the old adage of "either conform to the system and suffer the restriction of rights and privileges, or cease to be a part of the system." The massive laws and policies set up to ensure respect, authority, and obedience to the law have become a part of the weaponry that students have used to protect their own rights. Students are turning to the very essence that controlled them for so long—the law. They have discovered that they have rights as citizens and as students. Consequently, administrators and teachers take care to provide a safe learning environment without infringing on students' rights.

Due Process

The Fourteenth Amendment states that, "no state shall abridge the privileges or immunities of citizens of the United States; nor shall any State deprive any person of life, liberty, or property, without due process of the law, nor deny to any person within its jurisdiction the equal protection of the law." The Fifth Amendment similarly states that a person "may not be deprived of life, liberty, or property without due process of law." Essentially, these two amendments guarantee any citizen of the United States the procedural rights granted them in the Constitution.

In relation to student rights, a precedent was set in *Dixon v. Alabama State Board of Education* in 1979. In this case, high school students were expelled or placed on probation for a "sit-in" at a lunch counter. The violation of due process involved the failure to give notice of charges and grant a hearing. As a result of this action, notices of charges and rights to a hearing are now part of the rights of a student prior to expulsion (Chandler, 1992).

Due process involves two areas: (a) procedural due process, which is concerned with fair procedures; and (b) substantive due process, which guarantees that no individual will be "deprived of life, liberty, or property for arbitrary reasons." Arbitrary means unreasonable, discriminatory, or based on vague rules. Before a student is deprived of any substantial liberty or property interest, there should be adequate notice and a hearing before an impartial body where the student's side of the dispute is heard. Instances involving cases of serious administrative action dictate the application of certain procedures: notification of the evidence to be used against the student, names of the witnesses testifying, and the facts of the witnesses' testimony. In addition, students have the right to cross-examine any witness, to present witnesses and evidence, to receive a record of the proceedings and findings of any hearing, as well as the right to appeal.

There are two instances in which due process is not a prerequisite. The first instance relates to the many trivial activities that occur in schools. In situations involving "minor infractions of rules or non-performance of required tasks," a wide scope of punishments may be administered. Punishments may range from being remanded to the principal's office, to brief detentions. The second circumstance exempting due process as a prerequisite pertains to emergencies in which educators must act quickly to preserve the safety of persons or property. In situations defined as emergencies, the only legal requirement is that fair procedures be followed as soon as practicable after removal of the danger or disruption.

School administrators must follow guidelines established by state laws and the Supreme Court. Even though the stipulations of student rights vary from state to state, the Fourteenth Amendment provides protection for all, but allows latitude for state level modification and logical application by school administrators.

Harassment

Harassment is defined as any unwanted behavior, either verbal or physical, that stigmatizes or victimizes an individual. In schools, harassment can take place in various forms. The three main types include:

(a) Quid Pro Quo, or the granting of something in exchange for something;

(b) a hostile environment that alters the educational climate; and

(c) related discrimination, wherein, someone in a supervisory position takes action to enhance an individual's status because of race or for sexual favors.

Students may be the target of harassment by teachers, administrators, other school personnel, parents, and members of their own peer group. Fortunately, Title VII of the 1964 Civil Rights Act and Title IX of 1972 Educational Amendment provide protection for students against harassment. By law, students are entitled to pursue their educational pursuits in a non-threatening and stress-free environment.

Searches

Does the Fourth Amendment of the Constitution protect students from strip searches, mass searches, searches of lockers, personal belongings/possessions, and automobiles? On January 15, 1985 in *New Jersey v. T.L.O.*, the Supreme Court held that the Fourth Amendment protects students from unreasonable searches by school officials. Weighing the student's privacy interest against the school's legitimate need to maintain a learning environment, the Court held that public school searches must be reasonable under all of the circumstances. This landmark decision established the constitutional standard for searches of individual students by school officials.

The "reasonable suspicion" requirement in T.L.O. provides a broad framework for judging the legality of school searches. A student may be searched by school officials when there is reasonable grounds for suspecting that the search will turn up evidence that the student has violated or is violating either the law or rules of the school. Courts will not tolerate searches based on a general suspicion that some law/school rule has been broken. Administrators bear the burden of establishing that a student's behavior creates a reasonable suspicion that a specific rule/law has been violated and that a search could reasonably produce evidence of that violation.

The key factors that must be considered in determining whether a school search was based on reasonable suspicion include:

a. student's age, history, and record in school;

b. prevalence and seriousness of the problem to which

the search was directed;

c. the need to make a search without delay and further investigation;

d. the value and reliability of the information to justify the search;

e. the school official's experience with the student; and

f. the experience of the school official involved with the type of problem to which the search was directed (Majestic, 1987).

In T.L.O. the Court did not rule on whether students have a legitimate expectation of privacy in school storage spaces like lockers and desks. As a rule, schools retain ultimate ownership of student lockers. Courts have generally upheld that students have no valid expectation of privacy in their lockers and, consequently, no right to Fourth Amendment protection when the locker is searched (Majestic, 1985).

The Fourth Amendment does not prohibit school officials from patrolling student parking lots or inspecting the outside of student cars. Reasonable suspicion must be present to justify a search of the inside of a car. On the other hand, school officials must reserve strip searches for serious offenses in which it is reasonably likely that contrabands have been concealed on the student's body.

Implications for Counselors

Students do have clearly established legal rights which are protected and secured by the Constitution. However, students may not be informed of those rights. Counselors are appropriate persons to provide information on student rights to students, teachers, administrators, and parents. Therefore, counselors must be armed with up-dated information on the latest court decisions and laws. The necessity for open communication and compliance with state laws and Supreme Court decisions is paramount.

There is a need for collaborative efforts of counselors and teachers to develop curriculum pertaining to human/student rights issues. This is an area that must remain in the conscious of all entities involved. Since students will be the ones impacted the most, counselors must provide individual counseling, classroom guidance, and small groups to help students develop assertiveness skills; provide opportunities for active participation in choice awareness and consequences; and help students recognize the differences between student rights and student responsibilities. Not only must students become knowledgeable enough to be able to act and respond at a given moment, they must become empowered to know what their rights are and the degree to which those rights may be forfeited.

References

Chandler, G. L. (1992). Due process rights of high school students. *The High School Journal, 75,* 137-143.

Majestic, A. (1985). Search and seizure in the schools: Defining reasonableness. *School Law Bulletin, 16,* 1-8.

Majestic, A. (1987). Principles of search and seizure in the public schools. *School Law Bulletin, 18,* 15-27.

Shepard, J. (1993). The fourth amendment and searches in the public schools. *School Law Bulletin, 24,* 1-12.

WDCN. (1993). *Sexual Harassment in the workplace.*

Zirkel, P. A., & Gluckman, I. B. (1985). Student searches revisited— What is the proper standard? *NASSP Bulletin, 69,* 117-120.

Canary C. Hogan, Ed.D., NCC, NCSC, LPC is a school counselor at Ewing Park Middle School in Nashville, Tennessee and adjunct associate professor at Tennessee State University.

2

At-Risk Students and Violence

Lina Giusti

Overview

In recent years we have grown more and more aware of and concerned with violence in the streets and in our homes. Cities, suburbs and small towns are often settings for gruesome acts of violence. In the last decade we have witnessed children and teachers being assaulted and killed in rates which have doubled in the last 30 years, going from 4.7 homicides per 100,000 in 1960 (U.S. Bureau of the Census, 1990) to 10 homicides per 100,000 in 1991 (FBI Uniform Crime Report, 1991). Perpetrators are getting younger and younger. Arrests for homicides among juveniles increased by 332% between 1965 to 1990. (FBI Uniform Crime Report, 1991)

Violence

As defined by Webster's Dictionary (1986), violence is "an exertion of physical force to injure or abuse." We can say that it is more than physical force; it is also a mental and psychological force or a combination of these forces that produces emotional, physical, and psychological injury to the person. Violence has directionality, frequency, and severity. Violence can be expressed inside or outside the individual. Self-violence can be seen in such behaviors as car accidents and even suicide. Violence toward others can be directed toward the system, organizations, and people, or a combination of these. In considering the frequency, we talk about how often the violent incidents occur: daily or sporadically. If we consider the severity of the event, we can measure the violent behavior as mild, moderate, or criminal, ranging from truancy to homicide.

Taking a close look at school violence, we found that students' opinions are more critical than parents' views regarding the issue of a safe and secure environment in the school building. More than one-third of junior high students (36%) and 34% of high school students believe their school does only a fair or a poor job of providing a safe environment in the school building.

A sizeable proportion of students and parents assess their school negatively with regard to the school's facilities, such as buildings and playgrounds. As with other aspects of the school environment, students are more critical than parents, and high school students are most likely to evaluate their school negatively. Two in five junior high students (40%) and 43% of high school students think that their school does only a fair or a poor job of maintaining the facilities. Parents of adolescents and younger children have similar views about their school's ability to maintain the physical facilities.

The Problem

Violence is a multidimensional problem. There are factors present such as poverty, racism, breakdown of the family, and inadequate societal support systems for working parents. All of these factors play roles in the staggering rates of violence. The world in which we raise our children is extremely violent.

Millions of children and teens are frequent witnesses to acts of aggression. They watch it, hear it, read it, and play with it. Violence is a major theme in television shows, movies, newscasts, music, sports, literature, and children's toys. It is rampant in many North American cities (Garbiano, et al., 1992; Kotlowitz, 1991) and is constantly present in families. Homes are the major place where our children learn violence and the socialization process at home, during the first five years, is instrumental in children learning this behavior. The socialization process provides a different standard for boys and girls.

There is considerable agreement among experts that, although human beings, particularly men as a group, have the potential for learning violent behavior, the environment can make the difference in terms of encouraging or discouraging such actions. Violence is best understood as developing out of the interaction between a biological potential and certain kinds of environmental reinforcement.

The enormous escalation of violence that Americans are experiencing also seems to coincide with the development of a vast system of communication technology. This culture of violence now plays a major role in socializing American young people, who spend more time being entertained by the media than they spend with parents, family, or in school. This situation may have led to the creation of a culture of violence of unprecedented dimensions.

Who are At-risk?

Ingersoll and Orr (1988), in an article dealing with adolescents at-risk, view adolescence as a period of "storm and stress." For some young people, adolescence is an extended period of struggle; for others, the transition is marked by alternating periods of struggle and quiescence. Adolescents are especially at-risk. Their ability to draw on effective, adaptive coping behavior risks comprising physical, psychological, or social health. Adolescence seems most descriptive of a period of development characterized by such terms as stressful, vulnerable, wandering, searching, and striving. Within this profile there are individuals who pass through this developmental process seemingly unscathed and those who, in an attempt to meet the challenges, either by choice or circumstance, are unable to deal effectively with these situations. The concept of choice related to the at-risk population is best viewed in terms of the selection of behaviors that will place individuals in danger based on the outcomes of those behaviors. It is their selected way of coping with some challenges placed in their path that differentiates at-risk individuals from their peers (Gross & Cappuzzi, 1989). The concept surrounding the term, "circumstance," relates to factors within the young person's environment over which he or she has little control but which play a fundamental role in separating out those individuals most at-risk.

Role of the School Counselor

Academic excellence for all students must be at the core for all violence prevention efforts. Learning, itself, can prevent violence. The critical thinking skills that come from school success are essential elements of the ability to stop, think about alternatives, analyze them, and select the best course of action.

The school counselor needs to be aware of the critical environments in their schools and know how to interact with those environments. Counselors as facilitators should use their counseling skills to inspire feelings of trust, credibility, and confidence from parents and children in the guidance and counseling process. As therapists, counselors should communicate caring and respect for the parents and their children in the process. Counselors as program developers and advocates should have a clear view of community programs and services, and should try to empower their constituents to deal efficiently and effectively with the environment on behalf of themselves and the community in general. Recognizing that school administrators cannot accept full responsibility for violence in the school and its surroundings, school counselors need to involve themselves in social change through political reform so as to improve the critical environments which contribute to the development of young people. Solutions to the problem of violence in the school must reach beyond the school. Society must address the different components and variables that affect the quality of life and wellness of our children, their parents, and the whole community.

Conclusion

The heterogeneous nature of the at-risk population demands varied approaches to meet each individual's unique needs. The reasons why some youth do not succeed in school and in their lives are as many as the individuals themselves. The interplay of these reasons add to the complexity of the problem. Three areas suggested by Hathaway et al. (1989) are:

> Home and family support for learning: including self-esteem, security, acceptance, communication, personal responsibility, drug and sexuality education, rest, leisure, nutrition, and realistic goals, among others.
>
> School climate, expectations, and culture: clear, high, and appropriate expectations for personal, social, behavioral, and academic performance; parental and community involvement and feedback on performance, including rewards and incentives.
>
> Community support: for learning, employment, and career opportunities; support for parents and parenting; support for parent and school values and expectations; involvement in, and support for, school programs and services.

These endeavors need collaborative efforts to remove barriers to learning and school success through parenting skill enhancement; mental, physical, and emotional health care; screening and referral; day care; job training; and work experience training and support. At-risk students and violence is a multidimensional, multifactorial problem that requires a school-community partnership. This is a challenge that we need to address right now if we want to save the human race.

References

FBI. (1975-1991). *Uniform Crime Report.* Washington, DC: Department of Justice.

Garbiano, J., Dubrow, N., Kostelny, K. & Pardo, C. (1992). *Children in danger: Coping with consequences of community violence.* San Francisco, CA : Jossey-Bass.

Gross, D., & Capuzzi, D. (1989). Defining youth at-risk. In D. Cappuzzi & D.Gross (Eds.), *Youth at-risk* (pp. 3-17). Alexandria, VA: AACD.

Ingersoll, G. M., & Orr, D. P. (1988). Adolescents at-risk. *Counselor and Human Development Journal, 20,* 1-8.

Kotlowitz, A. (1991). *There are no children here. The story of two boys growing up in the other America.* New York: Doubleday.

U.S. Bureau of the Census. (1990). *Statistical abstracts of the United States.* Washington, D.C.: Author.

Lina Giusti, Ph.D., is a retired counselor educator who resides in Isla Verde, Puerto Rico. She was the 1995-1996 North Atlantic Region Chair for the American Counseling Association.

3

Conflict Management

Doris Rhea Coy

Overview

Conflicts are an inevitable part of living. Recorded human history notes how people have resolved conflicts by overcoming or overpowering their opponents. We attribute the concept of "winners and losers" to the need for people to control resources necessary for their survival or that of their families or tribe. The concept could also be related to the perpetuation of patriarchal societies where, even today, "stronger" men dominate "weaker" men and women. Perhaps our society follows the theory of evolution here; being strong and successful is valued over being different or less productive. The notion of winners and losers, or domination versus subjugation, is ingrained into modern culture so deeply that even leisure activities reflect this "all or nothing" mental paradigm. Competitive sports are valued in our society as character building, yet, they further reinforce the notion that winning is better than losing and cooperation between opponents has no place on the playing field (Todey, 1992).

There is increasing evidence to show that some ancient civilizations were much more advanced in their socialization practices than first thought. It is believed that our first archaeologists translated their findings into terms that fit with their personal experience. Stone figures and drawings, or insignificant cultic statues, are now thought to have been created to illustrate religious rites and to denote human understanding of these symbols to the environment (Todey, 1992).

The study of history often emphasizes conflict, battles, conquests, and struggles and deemphasizes people who lived in partnership where collaboration and cooperation were emphasized toward the development and enhancement of the people as a whole. No civilization has been without conflict but the methods used to deal with conflict vary significantly upon the culture of the people involved. People who adopt an attitude of "win/win vs win/lose" approach a problem quite differently. Modern society promotes the "win/lose" mentality, a position at odds with many ancient partnership societies which focused on promoting humankind rather than inventing weapons intended to dominate and overpower. The arts were nurtured, they invented architectural principles that incorporated beauty with function, promoted education, and craftsmanship. Children were raised by the community and peaceful coexistence was commonplace (Todey, 1992).

The very thing that made those ancient peacemakers so advanced also caused their demise. Because they were peace loving, they built no fortresses, had no weapons of war, and were unprepared for the attitude (win/lose) of the nomadic aggressors who conquered their lands and enslaved their peoples. The technologies that exist today are far beyond what the ancient world could ever have conceived. The world has become too small and too fragile for human mistreatment of the environment or each other (Todey, 1992).

The Nature of Conflict

What is conflict management? It is the peaceful negotiation process that takes place when two disputing parties are dedicated to the resolution of a mutual problem.

First, let us attempt to understand the nature of conflicts, then look at strategies for managing and resolving them. Conflict builds both within (internal) and outside (external) of us. Internal conflicts occur when opposing forces demand that we do something to provide satisfaction. External conflicts occur because the world is comprised of other people. My needs and values conflict with the needs and values of others (Sorenson, 1992).

Conflict exists when there are differences in beliefs, assumptions, information, opinions, needs, goals, ideas, and values. Conflict will occur in the friendliest of groups. It is a natural part of any relationship but it can weaken or strengthen the relationship. It can result in aggression or mutual understanding. We should be careful not to avoid conflicts or to resolve them too soon but we need to explore our differences to better understand ourselves and others (Sorenson, 1992).

How to Conduct Conflict Management

Jane Todey in *How to Conduct Conflict Management Training for School Personnel* lists the following roles of the conflict manager:
1. Restate disputants' explanations of the conflict.
2. Ask disputants to begin to restate the other person's

positions, feeling statements, etc.
3. Make sure that the problem is broken down if there is more than one part.
4. Make sure that a solution is found to each part of the problem.
5. Be skilled in the use of "I"-messages, active listening, and affirming positive behavior / responses by disputants.

The steps to be utilized in resolving a conflict are:
1. Take time to cool off and find a conflict manager (a disinterested person) to help.
2. Both disputants agree to the rules of:
   a. no putdowns
   b. no interruptions
3. Both disputants agree to try to solve the conflict.
4. Both disputants take turns explaining their position.
5. Both disputants take turns explaing how this effects them or how they feel about the conflict.
6. Both disputants are required to brainstorm solutions.
7. One or more solutions are agreed upon.
8. If necessary, friends are notified that the conflict has been resolved so that problems do not persist.

The outline suggested by Don L. Sorenson, Ph.D. in his book *Conflict Resolution and Mediation for Peer Helpers* is as follows:

Basic Framework for Mediating a Conflict
1. Select a location - privacy is essential to insure confidentiality
2. Prepare location - a table with three chairs. Arrange the furniture so everyone can see each other without difficulty. Blank copies of any forms you will use and pens.
3. Welcome - welcome participants and thank them for coming. Introduce yourself; ask participants to say their names. Decide how to address each other.
4. Orientation - Review key concepts about mediation with participants.
5. Ground Rules for Mediation - Review ground rules for mediation. Have participants sign the ground rules form.
6. Gather Information - Decide who should share first. Summarize what you heard. Ask person to identify his/

her feelings. Clarify feelings by identifying them as pleasant, unpleasant or both. Ask other person to describe what happened. Ask person to identify his/her feelings. Clarify feelings by identifying them as pleasant, unpleasant or both. Summarize what you hear, highlighting points of agreement as well as disagreement.

7. Confirm the Positions - Check with both individuals to see if they understood what the other said. Ask each person to restate what they heard the other person say.
8. Generate Options - Ask each participant what he/she each might do to resolve the conflict. Generate other possibilities.
9. Resolving - Which option might be further explored? Discuss alternatives and their consequences. What can be done to avoid similar conflicts in the future?
10. Closing - Respect rules of confidentiality concerning the session. May be appropriate to sign an agreement for implementing the solution.

The ideal group of individuals to teach about peaceful co-existence is children. By instilling in them the idea that conflict is normal, but can be resolved in a peaceful way, may bring about a nation of adults that believe in the same idea.

Resources

Learning the process of conflict management requires reading and experience. Many books are available on the topic, as are training sessions offered by groups that promote peaceful existence. The following resources are listed to assist you as you pursue this topic.

Creative Conflict Resolution by William Kriedler
Conflict Resolution in the Elementary Class Room by Barbara Porro
Children's Creative Response to Conflict
Peaceworks: Peacemaking Skills for Little Kids by Dr. Seuss
Six Thinking Hats by Edward DeBono
Learning the Skills of Peacemaking by Naomi Drew
Resolve by the Center for Creative Justice

Conclusion

School counselors, with the proper training and experience, have the skills to be leaders in conflict management. They may serve as members of school improvement teams planning for conflict prevention, professional development trainers for the faculty and staff, facilitators in solving conflict, classroom guidance instructors, and group counselors. Ideally, conflict resolution should start in elementary school where children can be taught how to handle conflict and promote peace.

References

Sorenson, D. L. (1992). *Conflict Management Training Activities.* San Francisco: The Community Boards, Inc.

Sorenson, D. L. (1992). *Conflict Resolution and Mediation for Peer Helpers.* San Francisco: The Community Boards, Inc.

Todey, J. (1992). *How to conduct conflict management training for school personnel.* Training for the American School Counselor Association.

Doris Rhea Coy is a counselor in private practice and consultant to business, education, government, and industry. She is a past president of the American Counseling Association and of the American School Counselor Association.

4

Learning Styles and School Counseling

Claudia Roels

Introduction

As schools undergo educational reform, specific teaching techniques are being researched and introduced in order to increase learning. Often schools, caught up in the novelty of a particular technique, do not take into consideration the variety of learning styles of students. Other research has brought to the forefront the importance of student learning styles, and there is evidence that a variety of approaches to learning maximizes the learning of all students.

School counselors not only need to be aware of learning styles in counseling interventions, they could also facilitate learning styles through comprehensive counseling programs, consultations with teachers, and staff inservices. As school counselors learn about various learning styles, they could become collaborators and consultants for teachers in helping to improve the learning process.

Implication for Improved Learning

It is essential for counselors to know and understand the definition of learning style. A comprehensive definition (adopted by a National Association of Secondary School Principles task force and composed of leading theorists in the field) is "...the composite of characteristic cognitive, affective, and physiological factors that serve as relatively stable indicators of how a learner perceives, interacts with, and responds to the learning environment" (Griggs, 1991). Curry (1987) describes a model with four layers: 1) personality dimensions; 2) information-processing; 3) social interaction; and 4) instructional preference. The personality models are represented by the *Myers-Briggs Type Indicator* (MBTI) and *True Colors* (which is a simplified version of the MBTI). The information-processing models include Kolb's *Learning Style*

Inventory, 4MAT system, and Gregoro's *Style Delineator*. The social interaction model is primarily represented by the Grasha-Reichmann *Student Learning Style Scale*. The multidimensional and instructional preference models are represented by Keefe & Monk's *Learning Style Profile* and Dunn & Dunn's *Learning Styles Model*. Other learning style models have been developed; the above models are most applicable to counseling and learning.

Learning style approaches have come under increasing scrutiny by educators, especially since other innovations have not worked satisfactorily, but learning style theory and approaches, since being introduced, have had a lasting effect on education. Analyzing the *Learning Style Inventory*, one educator criticized the ability of young students to formulate their learning needs better than the teacher's ability to assess those student needs. Another educator speculated on general approaches to learning-style-based education, recommending that teachers should assess students' learning styles rather than students self reporting their styles. Although criticisms have occurred, the fact remains that "...several well designed and carefully conducted studies verify that students are capable of accurately indicating the ways in which they will achieve best" (Dunn, Dunn &that Price, 1981).

School counselors have historically used personality assessments in career planning. Expanding their knowledge of assessment into the arena of learning styles, school counselors could become the primary school personnel to facilitate more effective student learning. "Students learn in different ways and, consequently, they require different ways of teaching for them to learn. Researchers say that more than 20 years of work on learning styles has confirmed that the way teachers present information can determine whether learning occurs" (*Education USA*, 1989). Using theoretical foundations with field validation evidence, the use of learning styles research and assessment will assist in the diagnosis, prescription, and improvement of attitudes toward learning.

Practical Applications of Learning Style Approaches

Through the use of comprehensive counseling programs, school counselors can conduct effective learning style activities. Selecting the most appropriate learning style approach may be perplexing. It is reassuring to discern that "no learning style is better-or worse-than any other style" (Griggs, 1991). Since most activities within comprehensive counseling programs involve classroom presentations, the variety of presentations could incorporate not only knowledge of learning styles, but also the understanding of individual differences, listening skills, note taking, time management, and test taking strategies. Even specific learning style approaches, such as the MBTI or True Colors, in conjunction with other assessment tools, can be helpful in a variety of populations, such as learning disabled groups, gifted students, and high risk students. In the course of classroom presentations, opportune times would arise for counselors to consult with teachers regarding student learning styles.

As counselors develop more alliances with parents and the community, they could be the vital link in communicating student learning preferences. Student learning preferences, or styles, affect how children learn, the classes they select, and their career choices. Counselor-conducted parent workshops could assist parents in understanding their child's individual learning preference or style.

It is important to recognize that everyone has learning style preferences, and these preferences are generalized to others (Griggs, 1991). With awareness of their own preferences, counselors would consult with teachers, establish communication links with parents, and provide specific information for appropriate classroom activities based on student learning styles. Then, with the understanding of student learning preferences, teachers, through a variety of instructional methodologies, will be able to more effectively accommodate unique student learning styles.

Conclusion

Schools face some major concerns: dropout issues, behavioral problems, and individual student crises such as violence and family disruption. The ever-increasing demands put upon school counselors, the necessity for accountability, and the need to maintain better programs and services, will revitalize the significant role that school counselors can play in the improvement of student learning. School counselor knowledge and expertise in using learning style assessments and curriculum application, will facilitate student learning, improve self-image, and enhance student success. School counselors, by the very nature of their educational preparation, are the most likely school personnel to deliver learning style activities. Through professional development activities which emphasize learning styles, school counselors will improve teacher student communication, enhance student educational growth, and establish the counselor as an integral player in promoting learning outcomes.

Resources

Davidman, L. (1981). Learning style: The myth, the panacea, the wisdom. *Phi Delta Kappan*, 641-645.

Dunn, R., Dunn, K., & Price, G.E. (1981). Learning styles: Research vs. opinion. *Phi Delta Kappan,* 645, 646.

Education USA. (1989). Special Issue. *Learning styles*. Arlington, VA: National School Public Relations Association.

Griggs, S. A. (1991). *Learning styles counseling*. Greensboro, NC: ERIC Counseling and Student Services Clearinghouse.

Humes, C. W. Career planning implications for learning disabled high school students using the MBTI and SDS-E. *The ASCA Counselor, 39*(5), 362-368.

Claudia Roels, MA, NCC is a school counselor at Moon Valley High School in the Glendale Union High School District, Phoenix, Arizona and was the ASCA Western Region Vice President, 1993-1995.

5

Attention Deficit/Hyperactivity Disorder and the School Counselor

Pamela Kaye Gabbard & Jackie M. Allen

Overview

An increasing number of children in schools are unable to focus on classroom lessons, sit still, listen to the teacher, complete their school work, and maintain satisfactory peer relationships. These at-risk children have become a common topic of magazine articles, newspaper reports, and television network specials. Many of these at-risk children have been diagnosed with the increasingly common childhood disorder of Attention-Deficit/Hyperactivity Disorder. It is estimated that one-out-of-five students in public schools is diagnosed with ADHD. School personnel and parents have become exhausted by the problems that these at-risk children present.

ADHD

Criteria for the diagnosis of ADHD are found in the Diagnostic and Statistical Manual of Mental Disorders-Fourth Edition (1994). Major characteristics of the disorder include inattention, hyperactivity, and impulsivity. The prevalence of ADHD in school children is about 3% to 5%. It is more common in males than females, with a sex ratio ranging from 4:1 in the general population to 9:1 in clinical settings. Usually the disorder, characterized by excessive motor activity, is noticed when children are toddlers. ADHD is not usually diagnosed until children are school age and the symptoms begin to interfere with their learning.

Behavior is not usually isolated in one setting and is noticeable across settings such as at home and at school. Parents report that when at home, children have more disruptive behavior, are noncompliant, and fail to pay attention. These children appear to be unable, rather than unwilling, to learn from their mistakes. In school, these students often blurt out answers, interrupt others, lose things, and engage in physically dangerous activities without considering the consequences. Thus, poor school performance is manifested in unfinished assignments, trouble following directions, fidgeting, excessive talking, and distraction by other classroom activities.

Any one of the previously listed behaviors is normal in childhood; rather, it is the degree of frequency and severity, the presence in more than one environment, and the developmental appropriateness of the behaviors that identifies an ADHD child from his/her peers. Students with ADHD are more likely than other children to have learning disabilities or to exhibit behavior disorders.

The etiology of ADHD is unknown. The disorder has been found to have a hereditary link in first-degree biological relatives of children with ADHD (DSM IV, 1994). Treatment may include behavior modification, cognitive therapy, medication, or a combination of the three. Ritalin has become the ADHD treatment of choice with 1.3 million children from the ages of 5 to 14 taking it regularly (Hancock, 1996). Counseling and family therapy are often necessary to help family members understand the behavior of their children.

A successful effort to understand and work with ADHD students requires the following factors:

1. Training and information about ADHD must be provided to all school personnel.
2. A collaborative team approach must be used to successfully meet students' needs.
3. Teachers must have commitment and willingness to work with individual children to meet their unique needs.
4. A structured environment must be established for the student.
5. A good working relationship must be established between home and school.
6. School support staff such as school counselors must be actively involved in monitoring and effectively modifying school climate to serve the needs of ADHD students.

The Role of the School Counselor

The school counselor is the advocate for the ADHD child. The school counselor not only has the appropriate training but also the personal commitment to student success. The school counselor is the model for other school staff as he/she encourages and supports specialized teaching strategies for the ADHD child in the classroom. The school counselor must also encourage and support professional development activites for the school staff. In making frequent contacts, such as a daily welcome with a smile, the school counselor can respond quickly to the special needs of ADHD students. As a member of the consultation team, the school counselor supports collaborative efforts.

When a consultation team is established, the school counselor joins the school psychologist and school social worker, with their knowledge in learning disabilities and ADHD, to provide suggestions for appropriate interventions. The ADHD student may receive services from the school counselor, such as group or individual counseling, behavior modification, and teacher consultation. Parent education is important for school success with ADHD children. The school counselor provides parents and staff educational strategies recommended for ADHD student needs. School counselors also act as resources, providing referrals to social agencies, educational resource teams, or community action groups.

The ADHD student needs specialized educational interventions and, sometimes, assessment. As the advocate for these students, the school counselor's role is to pursue appropriate interventions for the student which may include 504 plans or special education placement, thus making the difference in the student's success in the school system.

Conclusion

Every student needs someone at their side: caring, protecting, encouraging, and listening. School counselors believe that children are the top priority in our schools, communities, and the nation. All school personnel must become advocates for ADHD students. The professional school counselor can help both parents and teachers meet the challenges of ADHD students.

References

American Psychiatric Association. (1994). Diagnostic and statistical manual of mental disorders. (4th ed.). Washington, DC: Author.

Bowley, B. A., & Walther, E. (1992). Attention deficit disorders and the role of the school counselor. *The Journal of Elementary School Guidance and Counseling.*

Gomez, K. M., & Cole, C. L. (1991). Attention deficit hyperactivity disorder: A review of treatment alternatives. *The Journal of Elementary School Guidance and Counseling.*

Parker, H. (1992). The ADD hyperactivity handbook for schools. Plantation, FL: Impact Publications, Inc.

Pamela Kaye Gabbard, is an elementary school counselor at Ballard County Elementary, Barlow, Kentucky. She served as the American School Counselor Association 1994-1996 Elementary Vice President.

Jackie M. Allen, former ASCA president 1993-1994, is a school counselor and school psychologist in the Fremont Unified School District, Fremont, California and lecturer/consultant with Allen Consulting Associates.

6

Multicultural Counseling and the School Counselor

Darryl T. Yagi

Multicultural Counseling: Challenges for the School Counselor

As a nation, our multicultural society fosters pluralism. Individuals from all walks of life, especially those youngsters who come from various ethnic and cultural groups, domestic and foreign, steadily pass through our classrooms and offices. Are trained school counselors prepared to be culturally responsive to the unique needs of students from cultural backgrounds far different than our own? In preparation for our schools, are school counselors ready to provide guidance programs that account for ethnic and cultural variables? In the delivery of a comprehensive counseling service, are school counselors addressing the developmental needs of students from culturally diverse backgrounds?

The American School Counselor Association's position statement on cross/multicultural counseling (1988) highlights the need for school counselors to become culturally responsive, to understand cultural diversity, and to provide multicultural counseling services. As an outgrowth of the position statement, the Human Rights Committee of the American School Counselor Association developed a cultural diversity inservice training guide for school counselors (1989), which provides both an awareness statement and training for cultural diversity.

School counselors help students to look within and to become knowledgeable about themselves. Before school counselors proceed to counsel others in a cultural context far different than their own, however, it is important to understand one's own cultural context. In order to have a multicultural perspective, the acknowledgement of the school counselor's "culture" is the first challenge. It is essential to recognize how the world is veiwed from a set of core values, which may be of a white, middle class, European culture. Equally consequential is the basic assumption about ethnic groups and the considerations for cultural stereotyping, bias, and prejudice. Although school counselor training may add value in a European/American context, school counselor preparation may be multiculturally counterproductive. Traditional school counseling preparation practices may be part of a framework that inherently does not take into account cultural differences. The challenge is to assess and acknowledge one's own cultural view and cultural assumptions.

Multicultural counseling recognizes cultural diversity. The acknowledgement of the cultural dynamics within individuals and groups, as well as between individuals and groups, is paramount to multicultural counseling. For example, within the Asian culture there are vast differences between ethnic groups, which are largely driven by history and generation, here and abroad. By developing an awareness of the culturally diverse student population in our schools, an understanding of cultural variables and values of students from culturally diverse backgrounds, and a repertoire of culturally responsive skills, the school counselor can address cultural issues that affect the developmental needs of children and youth.

In *Counseling for Diversity, A Guide for School Counselors and Related Professionals,* (Lee, 1995) developmental school counseling with a multicultural perspective is presented. In essence, consideration of student development must be related to the cultural context of the individual. Cultural differences give rise to variables, such as kinship, roles and status, sex-role socialization, language, religion/spirituality, and ethnic identity, which impact student development (Lee, 1995). The culturally responsive school counselor must be mindful not to superimpose mainstream criteria of student development on a culturally diverse student body.

Although the range of cultures is enormous, the following brief examples suggest the kinds of cultural issues to which school counselors must be prepared to respond. Counselors must be ready to develop guidance programs and be able to deliver a comprehensive counseling service to address the developmental needs of students from culturally diverse backgrounds.

The largest ethnic group within our schools is the nation's Hispanic children and youth. The Hispanic population includes individuals from Mexico, Central America and South America, as well as people from Cuba, Puerto Rico, and the Dominican Republic. Cultural issues of family, gender, role, religion, and identity affect some of the unique needs of the Hispanic students. Acculturation, immigration, and economic variables are additional social factors which must be considered in the counseling process. Language acquisition, school achievement, and career development among Hispanic youth indicate a need for a stronger guidance program.

The next largest ethnic group in the school setting is the African American youth. Family, gender, role, religion, identity, and dialect are some of the cultural factors which need to be acknowledged while counseling these youth. A long history of racism and economic deprivation affect the development of the African American youth. Group counseling, mentoring, and role modeling, as part of the guidance program, can not only affect self-esteem, but school performance as well.

The fastest growing ethnic group in our classrooms consists of the Asian American student. Asian Americans' cultural origin include such countries as China, Japan, Philippines, Korea, Vietnam, Cambodia, and Laos. There are strong cultural elements of family, extended family, gender differentiation, role delineation, religion, tradition, custom, language, and identity. Acculturation, immigration, and language are factors to consider in meeting the developmental needs of Asian American children and youth. The "model minority" myth and subsequent high expectations often creates a burden on the Asian American student. Equally stressful is the great expectation for high academic achievement imposed by the parents, school, and society. Cultural variables and communication styles affect individual and group counseling processes.

A significant, but a smaller ethnic group in the school environment is the Native American student. A heterogeneous group, Native Americans are culturally diverse in family, gender, role, tradition, custom, language, and identity. In addition, the history of racism and economic depression affect the development of the Native American child and youth. Cultural factors favor family counseling, peer counseling, and group counseling. Alcohol prevention, dropout prevention, and self-esteem building need to be an integral part of the guidance program.

Multicultural counseling is inclusive of the 3 C's: counseling, consultation, and coordination of a comprehensive, developmental school counseling program and service. The culturally responsive school counselor uses acquired awareness, knowledge, and skills in a multicultural context to meet the academic, career, and personal/social developmental needs of students from culturally diverse environments.

Recommended School Counselor Action

School counselors face the major challenge of multicultural counseling with children and youth from culturally diverse backgrounds. Part of the challenge is to demonstrate an understanding and appreciation for cultural diversity. School counselors can promote cultural inclusion within our schools and multicultural curriculum in our classrooms. In order to enhance student development, there must be a level of knowledge of how students are affected by cultures. Knowledge of cultural dynamics can provide culturally responsive counseling during cultural conflicts. School counselors can develop, implement, and evaluate culturally responsive guidance programs, based upon a needs assessment and upon systematic strategies.

A culturally responsive, comprehensive counseling service in the schools would include multicultural classroom guidance activities, cross/multicultural consultation, and coordination of resources within the cultural milieu. School counselors would combine their cultural knowledge and responsive skills to implement a comprehensive counseling service which is culturally relevant. For professional growth, school counselors must continue to seek professional development in order to achieve multicultural competence.

Conclusion

Multicultural counseling is a major challenge for the school counselor. The challenge begins by each of us assessing one's own cultural views and acknowledging one's own cultural assumptions. School counselor awareness of cultural differences and understanding of cultural variables are critical in responding to cultural issues that affect the developmental needs of children and youth from culturally diverse backgrounds.

It is clear that in our ever-changing schools, the culturally responsive counselor must provide a developmental, comprehensive guidance and counseling program which addresses the cultural relevancy and multicultural context of the school environment. Through multicultural counseling, the school counselor can promote cultural inclusion in our schools and foster cultural pluralism within our society. This is not only a challenge, but is also a responsibility and opportunity for school counselors to affect positive, constructive change within our multicultural schools.

References

American School Counselor Association. (1988). *Position statement: Cross/multicultural counseling.* Alexandria, VA: Author.

American School Counselor Association. (1989). *Cultural diversity: In-service training guide for school counselors.* Alexandria, VA: Author.

Baker, S. (1995). Becoming Multiculturally Competent Counselors. *The School Counselor, 42,* 179.

Lee, C. (1995). School Counseling and Cultural Diversity. In C.C. Lee (Ed.), *Counseling for diversity, A guide for school counselors and related professionals,* (pp. 8-9). Needham Heights, MA: Allyn and Bacon.

Darryl T. Yagi, M.A., NCC, NCCC, NCSC, MFCC is a school counselor at Casa Grande High School in Petaluma, California.

7

Counseling Native Students

Sarah C. Greenfield

You are a Native* student, waiting to see a counselor for the first time. This counselor will be of a different race or tribe. What do you want them to know about you?

"I'm sitting here, wondering, worrying. My heart is pounding like a powwow drum. Why am I here? Why not my family? Why see a stranger? I've tried, but I can't really talk with my family. Maybe I can talk with this stranger, this counselor. Maybe this person will know what to do."

"But how can I trust this person? How can I trust someone who is not family, who does not have a clan, who is not like me? Will they respect me? Will they respect my ways?"

"I brought Grandma along. She said this is a family problem, so I should bring some family. But is that OK? And Grandma is wearing her traditional dress. I love Grandma, but is that okay, her wearing traditional clothes? Will the counselor welcome us both?"

"And what about my English? I don't speak perfect English. Grandma doesn't speak English at all. Will this counselor hear what I'm saying? Will this person understand my silence . . . when I don't speak at all?"

"We went to see the medicine man. We made arrangements for a ceremony. But I'm here, too. Will it help to be here? I feel so lost, not knowing what to do."

You are the counselor, waiting to see this Native student for the first time. What do you want to know?

---

* *In this digest, "Native" refers to Native American Indians and Alaskan Natives.*

Recommendations for Experiencing Native America

Counselors should learn about Native cultures through: (a) visiting reservations and cultural centers (remembering that you need an invitation to visit private homes or to attend ceremonies); (b) attending rodeos, powwows, and dances; (c) talking and consulting with Native people; (d) investigating tribal history, beliefs and values, current tribal organization, and the tribe's family structure, gender and age roles; and (e) taking courses and becoming familiar with Native heroes, heroines, and famous contemporary Native people.

Values

Great differences exist between Native values and those of mainstream America. Each culture's values make each people unique.

Mainstream American values	*Traditional Native values*
individualism, nuclear family	extended family, group, clan
emphasis on youth	respect for elders
competition	cooperation
knowledge is good	some things cannot be known
keep	give
time consciousness	lack of time consciousness
future orientation	present orientation
doing	being
analytic (sequential, linear)	holistic
conquest of nature	harmony with nature

Native Spirituality and Healing

Living in harmony with tribal values and beliefs is very important for traditional Native peoples. Reverence for nature (in all its forms) and the spiritual nature of all life are central to the beliefs of most tribes. Mind, body, spirit, and nature are perceived as one process, with little separation between religion, medicine, and the activities of daily life. All things are connected.

Traditional Natives believe that every individual shares responsibility for making themselves well or unwell (except when witchcraft has been used). The universe is filled with enormously powerful forces holding the potential for good and evil. If the balance between good and evil is upset, people get sick. (For example,

Navajos consult a hand trembler or crystal gazer to diagnose the problem causing the disharmony, and then go to the appropriate singer—hatathlii—for a ceremony to treat the problem and promote healing.) Health results from having a harmonious relationship with nature. To stay healthy, stay in balance.

Many Native rituals and ceremonies are used for healing: sweat lodge, vision quest, medicine wheel, talking circle, pipe ceremony, peyotism, ritual dancing, and sun dance. Counselors working with Natives would be wise to learn about local healing ceremonies.

Specific Techniques for Counseling Native Students

Remember that each student is unique and must be appreciated as an individual. Meet each student as a person, not a case.

- Put the student at ease.
- When using a handshake, use a soft handshake, not a firm, aggressive one. (Some Natives may not want to be touched at all—handshakes are not necessarily Native.)
- Be accepting when the student brings a family member or friend.
- Determine if you need a translator.
- Keep the atmosphere casual, relaxed, and non-threatening.
- Communicate that there are no demands to behave in a certain way or talk a certain amount.
- Pay particular attention to nonverbal communication, observing the student's behavior, noting tone of voice, pace of speech, and degree of eye contact, then subtly match them to increase rapport.
- Generally avoid eye contact. (Avoiding eye contact shows respect for authority.)
- Use silence, restatement, and general lead.
- While facilitating easy conversational exchange, become comfortable with long pauses in conversation; use silence as a positive act, remembering that silence is also communication.
- Use humor (e.g., dry sense of humor, teasing)
- Keep the counseling short-term, ahistorical, directive, relational, authoritative, problem-focused, and action-oriented.
- Focus on the present more than on the past or the future.
- Emphasize practical problem-solving.
- Describe alternatives, options, and choices.
- Suggest solutions, then let the student decide on a course

of action, realizing that the student knows what is best to do.

- Because Natives learn through observation, use modeling and role-playing.
- Use non-verbal interactions such as play and art.
- Be sensitive to the student's frame of reference; accept and work within the student's belief system for promotiong change or healing.
- Use the Native's family as a resource.
- Learn as much as possible about the Native culture and specific local tribes, and then forget it in the live encounter with the student.

Because most contemporary Native people are a product of both their own indigenous culture and Western culture, blending counseling methods with traditional healing techniques may be your best therapeutic intervention.

In this digest we have looked at a Native student's concerns while waiting to see the counselor, ways to experience Native America, contrasts between Native and mainstream American values, traditional Native spirituality and healing, and some specific techniques for counseling Native students.

The Dakota/Lakota (Sioux) people end all their prayers, public gatherings, and ceremonies with the words, "mitakuye oyasin," meaning

"We are all related." In all things, be as with relatives. In this same spirit, I end with these same words;

Mitakuye oyasin. I say this in the name of all my relations.

References

Dufrene, P. M., and Coleman, V. D. (1994). Art and healing for Native American Indians. *Journal of Multicultural Counseling and Development, 22*(3), 145-152.

Garrett, J. T., & Garrett, M. W. (1994). The path of good medicine: Understanding and counseling Native American Indians. *Journal of Multicultural Counseling and Development, 22*(3), 134-144.

Hammerschlag, C. A. (1988). *The dancing healers.* San Francisco: Harper and Row. 170p.

Heinrich, R. K., Corbine, J. L., & Thomas, K. R. (1990). Counseling Native Americans. *Journal of Counseling and Development.* 69(2), 128-133.

Herring, R. D. (1989). Counseling Native American children: Implications for elementary school counselors. *Elementary School Guidance & Counseling, 232*(4), 272-281.

Rhodes, R. W. (1994). *Nurturing learning styles in Native American students.* Hotevilla, Arizona: Sonwai Books.

Ross, A. C. (1989). *Mitakuye Oyasin: "We are all Related."* Ft. Yates, ND: Bear.

Thomason, T. C. (1991). Counseling Native Americans: An introduction for non-Native American counselors. *Journal of Counseling and Development, 69*(4), 321-327.

Thornbrugh, C., & Fox, S. J. (1988). Bridging the challenging years: Tips for working with American Indian teenagers. ERIC Clearinghouse on Rural Education and Small Schools, Las Cruces, NM, 91p. ED295773.

Sarah C. Greenfield, Ph. D., is a school counselor at Chinle Junior High School, in the Chinle Unified School District #24, in Chinle (Navajo Nation), Arizona.

8

Counseling for High Skills

Kenneth B. Hoyt, Judith K. Hughey & Kenneth F. Hughey

Overview

The emerging information-oriented, high-skills, occupational society makes *some* form of postsecondary education essential for almost all persons seeking to enter the primary, as opposed to the secondary, labor market (Drucker, 1994, Marshall & Tucker, 1993). Jobs requiring one to two years of postsecondary occupational education are predicted to increase by thirty-four percent—faster than for any other category of education—between 1992 and 2005 *(Occupational Outlook Quarterly*, Spring, 1994).

School counselors have often been accused of spending most of their time helping the 30% of high school youth who will some day be four-year college graduates, not the 70% who won't (National Center on Education and the Economy, 1990). A great need exists to help school counselors increase their interest, ability, and commitment in helping non-four-year-college-bound high school leavers pursue some form of postsecondary sub-baccalaureate occupational education.

In 1993, a three-year 3.3 million dollar effort to demonstrate how this need can be met was awarded to Kansas State University by the DeWitt Wallace - Reader's Digest Fund. The project was entitled "Counseling for High Skills" (CHS). The purpose of this article is to describe the nature, current status, and future plans of the CHS Project.

Description of the CHS Project

CHS operates from a basic assumption that today's high school students will be inclined to consider enrolling in a postsecondary, one-to-two year program if they have access to answers—provided by the institution's current and former students—to their most frequently asked questions concerning attendance at such institutions. Thus, the basic data collection instruments contain items related to those questions. The initial data collection instrument is administered to current students in specific programs in each institution. The follow-up instrument is administered to these same students six months after the date they indicate they plan to leave the institution. Data collected using both instruments constitute a "customer satisfaction" approach to helping high school students answer the question "Is this a good program for *me*?". Because it involves answering questions most frequently asked by high school students and because data are collected from present and former students rather than from the institution itself, this represents quite a different approach to helping high school students consider postsecondary education options.

The CHS project is carried out as a "partnership" arrangement with the State division of the American School Counselor Association (ASCA) in twelve demonstration states, plus the District of Columbia. In each demonstration state, the ASCA Division State President has appointed one of the Division's members to serve as Project State Coordinator. The Project State Coordinator, in turn, has selected another ASCA State Division member to serve as "Director of Data Collection" (DDC) for each postsecondary institution invited by the Project State Coordinator to participate in the project. Finally, each DDC selects yet another member to serve as "Data Collection Facilitator" (DCF) and actually collect data from present and former students in a specific program in a specific institution. Project Staff persons have prepared a data collector's administration manual for use in collecting data in a standardized manner. However, the data collectors are all practicing school counselors. By operating in this manner, the CHS Project becomes a vehicle by which school counselors accept responsibility both for (a) collecting data *they* need and (b) *changing their own knowledge, attitudes, and commitments* toward helping youth consider various options available to them in postsecondary sub-baccalaureate educational programs.

Each participating postsecondary institution appoints an Institutional Representative (IR) from its staff. The IR and the DDC selected for each specific institution work together in selecting particular programs where data are to be gathered and for arranging specific data collection schedules. Programs are selected for data collection based, in large part, on the number of currently enrolled students under age 25. A minimum of 15 such persons is sought for each program where data are to be collected. Data are generated only from these students in an attempt to provide high school students with answers provided by other young persons, not older adults.

All completed data collection instruments are sent to the American College Testing Program (ACT) for processing. ACT first compiles all data collected from students in each participating institution and sends it to the institution for approval. If the institution does not want a particular bit of data transmitted to ASCA State Division members, it can request those data be deleted from reports sent to such persons. The remaining data collected from the students in each selected program in each participating institution are then organized around answers to the major questions asked by high school students and then placed on a special computer disk for use by counselors in each participating state. One set of data are supplied representing students in each program in each institution.

A free copy of the special computer disk, prepared for each participating state, is provided to each ASCA State Division member who attends a special staff development session aimed at helping counselors learn how to best use the data in counseling high school students and in working with parents, teachers, and other community persons. When the follow-up data have been collected, ACT processes those data, adds it to the initially collected data, and prepares a new computer disk, which is also submitted free to each ASCA State Division member who attends another staff development session conducted by project staff.

Project evaluation has been contracted by the DeWitt Wallace - Reader's Digest Fund to an independent third party evaluator—MPR, Inc. in Berkeley, California. Preliminary pre-treatment data have been accumulated from several thousand high school students. The eventual evaluation program will include an assessment of the effect of counselor possession and use of the CHS materials on future plans of high school students. To date we have found no reason to suspect evaluation results will be negative in nature. On the contrary, things appear to be going well—at least up to now.

The project is now in its second year of funding. Third year funding is due to begin December 1, 1995. Funds from this grant are currently scheduled to expire November 30, 1996.

Future Plans

As of March 31, 1995, initial data had been collected from approximately 18,000 postsecondary students enrolled in about 800 programs in about 230 institutions in the 13 participating states with about 750 school counselors involved as a Project State Coordinator, a DDC, or a DCF. The first follow-up attempts were initiated in January, 1995. While, of course, much of the total follow-up effort remains to be done, usable replies have already been received from 850+ former students.

The future of CHS will obviously be dependent on producing and reporting good evaluation results. Assuming positive evaluations are produced, three major kinds of plans have been proposed. First, problems exist related to sharing data with school counselors who are not now members of the ASCA State Division in each participating state. Grant funds, which are required to share the computer disks with all others on an "upon request" basis, do not now exist. Neither do funds exist that are required for use in professional development sessions aimed at showing those who receive the disks how best to use them in working with students, parents, other educators, and the general public. At present, the most viable solutions to solving these problems appear to be to either (a) allow ACT to sell the computer disks at a price worthwhile for them or (b) allow each participating ASCA State Division to sell computer disks to counselors who are not now members of the ASCA State Division. A third alternative could conceivably be found if the computer disks were made available to each state Department of Education in each of the 13 participating states along with authority to make copies for school counselors throughout the State. No final decisions have been made in these matters to date.

A second major problem has to do with how and when we will be able to extend the CHS Project so that it covers partnerships with ASCA State Divisions in all 50 states and territories. To do this in ways compatible with our current approaches may well cost as much as 15- 20 million dollars. These funds could obviously come from another large funding agency. They may, of course, come from state funds that become available under existing federal legislation such as Tech Prep, the School-to-Work Opportunities Act, or the 1995 version of the Carl D. Perkins legislation. It is even possible that arrangements could be made to allow individual community colleges to arrange for school counselors in their key feeder schools to collect and use CHS-type data using our data collection instruments and procedures. In such circumstances, the community college and/or the feeder high schools would have to make financial arrangements with ACT to process and report the data. The CHS Project Staff at Kansas State University is currently available to help those trying to make arrangements for extending CHS efforts in these ways.

A third major problem to be solved can be seen by observing that, as of today, the average age of community college students is

30+ years. Many community college students are persons who came out of high school with few, if any, specific job skills. Typically, such persons have found and held jobs in the secondary labor market on numerous occasions. Ten to fifteen years after leaving high school, increasing numbers of these persons have recognized that, if they want to enter and progress in the *primary* labor market, they will need to return to some kind of educational institution that will provide them with the specific job skills they need. The CHS data are currently being collected only from postsecondary students and former students under age 25. This is because of DeWitt Wallace - Reader's Digest Fund policies that largely restrict use of grant funds to projects aimed at helping K-12 youth. A huge need exists to extend the CHS operations so as to include students 25 years old and older, in addition to those under age 25. CHS activities to date have demonstrated how such data collection could occur. It will require another major funding source if these kinds of data are to be collected.

Conclusion

Counseling for High Skills (CHS) is a demonstration grant awarded to Kansas State University by the DeWitt Wallace - Reader's Digest Fund. It is aimed at demonstrating the feasibility of collecting and using a "customer satisfaction" approach to helping high school youth consider postsecondary educational opportunities at the sub-baccalaureate level. It is also aimed at demonstrating how the knowledge, attitudes, and commitments of school counselors can be changed in ways that lead them to provide better and more appropriate help to high school students for whom some kind of postsecondary occupational education would be appropriate.

Based on its first 1 1/2 years of operation, it is concluded that CHS is, indeed, a needed vehicle appropriate for use in helping today's school counselors better meet the career development needs of the 70% of today's high school students who will never be four-year college graduates. It should find some way of operating on a continuing basis.

References

Drucker, P.E. (1994, November). The age of social transformation. *The Atlantic Monthly,* pp. 53 - 80.

Marshall, R., & Tucker, M. (1993). *Thinking for a living.* New York: Basic Books.

National Center on Education and the Economy. (1990). *America's choice: High skills or low wages.* Rochester, N.Y.: Author.

Occupational outlook quarterly, (Spring, 1994). Occhart. 38(1). p. 53.

9

Student Transitions: Moving From Fear to Opportunity

Jan Olsen & Paula Crandall

Overview

As a group of new students stopped at the counseling office during their building tour, their faces reflected a myriad of emotions; exuberant smiles full of enthusiasm, blank stares in denial and wide-eyed looks filled with fear and dread. So many feelings...so many levels...so many changes....

This chapter will address basic insights and understandings about student transitions. These understandings can assist school counselors in addressing the developmental transitional needs of students and their impact on parents and faculty. Additionally, we will examine and provide strategies for managing transition on both a programmatic and student level.

The Nature of Change

Due to the complexity of society, students encounter more rapid changes than ever before witnessed. Changing family structures, increased mobility, and evolving employment patterns have had a dramatic impact on school children. Educational changes, including the restructuring of schools and school curriculums, and the location and configuration of schools add to the new dimension of transitions children must face.

The ancient adage "the only thing permanent in life is change" is so true for children and youth in our society. In a constantly shifting world, living with change need not imply insecurity for students, but rather ways of developing new forms of security must be addressed. Change is a process that is a constant force throughout one's life and must be dealt with in a rational manner. If change is managed, it can be seen as positive development. However, unmanaged change can result in anxiety which interferes with learning, and peer and family relationships.

Although students sometimes have no control over the changes in their lives, they CAN have control in the manner in which they manage change. Transition, the reorientation to a change, allows students to take charge.

Stages of Change

Students move through four phases in every transition. Some may quickly move from phase to phase, while others may become "stuck" and need assistance. Effective programing can help a student move through the various stages of transition resulting in improved academic performance and enhanced relationships with parents as well as faculty.

Stage one: DENIAL (danger stage)

> During the denial stage, students tend to focus on the past and a bargaining takes place to keep things the way they were. Students may also appear apathetic.

Stage two: RESISTANCE (danger stage)

> During the resistance stage, the impending change becomes real and personal. The students wonder where they stand in this process and how it will affect them. Behavioral traits in this stage may include not sleeping at night, or a display of anger through fighting and withdrawal. Academic performance may decline.

Stage three: EXPLORATION (confusion stage)

> Students at the exploration stage have an over-abundance of information related to their transition... so much that it may cause an overload. Students may experience feeling frustrated and confused. The student may lose his/her ability to focus when communicating or performing tasks. At this stage, students appear to be disorganized and forgetful. Many tasks are begun, but left unfinished, however, students may put forth a good effort. Some youth have described this stage as "treading water" and one of non-accomplishment.

Stage four: COMMITMENT: (accomplishment stage)

> Feelings of students in this final stage are ones of satisfaction and belonging. They feel a part of the structure and can sort out what is and isn't important. In a behavioral sense, students are more focused. As a result, more tasks are accomplished and

academic performance increases. In addition, relationships are more open, honest, and fluid.

Support Strategies For Successful Transitions

A Comprehensive School Counseling program will have integral components that assist students in the development of age appropriate skills. In order for students to make positive transitions in their lives, the following student competencies must be evident in the school counseling program:

(1) identification and expression of feelings
(2) assertiveness
(3) the ability to access pertinent information
(4) an understanding that change itself is neutral ; how students manage change makes it a positive or negative event
(5) the ability to set up their own support system

There are numerous activities that can assist students through the various stages of transition. The following is a list and brief description of some helpful activities that practicing professional school counselors have shared.

New Student Groups : Led by peer facilitators, students who have moved into a new school district can explore feelings of loss, gain information about the workings of their new school, and lay groundwork for a strong support system.

Orientation Programs: Parent/student meetings and school tours followed by a question/answer period can take the edge off of entering a new school. Slide or video programs depicting the student's new surroundings are helpful prior to visitations.

Individual Counseling: Aside from an intake interview and "welcome to our school," new students will require additional follow-up to assure a smooth transition is taking place.

Pen Pals and Student Newspapers: Pair students of an elementary class with students from a middle school and write letters, exchanging questions and comments about moving to middle school. A student newspaper could also answer questions for new students as well as introduce them to the student body through a welcome article.

The Buddy System: Pair a new student with a peer. Instant help, directions, and the beginning of a support system are in place.

Happy Hellos: The school intercom is an ideal place to welcome new students and give positive announcements.

Family Groups: Many schools have Teacher/Advisor groups,

Home Rooms or Home bases that are small and "family-like," promoting support and a sense of belonging to new students through discussion or activities.

Student Ambassadors: Two High School Freshmen are assigned to an eighth-grade home room to share their impressions of high school as they experience it. This may occur once a quarter.

Personal Essay: Reflecting on their years in a particular grade-level building, students write a culminating essay dealing with their accomplishments and their own development.

Review Cumulative Record: Individually or in small groups, students are able to identify where they have been in order to determine goals for their future.

Conclusion

Transition, whether it means moving to a new school or dealing with a new lifestyle, is inevitable. It can be disturbing when forced upon us, or stimulating when controlled by us. With assistance from professional school counselors, students in transition will be able to utilize choices and thus impact their futures.

References

Carr, T., & Schmidt, J. (September, 1994). Who's afraid of the ....?: A survey of eighth grade concerns. *The School Counselor, 42,* 66-72.

Downing, J., Haywood, N.,& Hish, W. (November, 1994). The cumulative record made easy. *The School Counselor, 45,* 167-169.

Prupas, B. (February, 1994) Using a student newsletter to teach problem-solving techniques to children. *Elementary School Guidance and Counseling,* 28 (3), 229-231.

Scott, C. D., & Jaffe, N. T. (1989). *Managing organizational change.* MenLo Park, CA: CRISP Publications.

Paula Crandell, NCC, NCSC, is a professional school counselor at LeMars Middle School, LeMars, IA and the ASCA Middle/Jr. High Vice President. Jan Olson, NCC, NCSC, is a professional school counselor at East High in Sioux City, IA and a past ASCA Secondary Vice President and 1994 ASCA Conference Chair. Ms. Crandell and Ms. Olson have a reputation for innovative program development and implementation.

10

Stages of Adolescents and Middlescents: Working with Parents and Teens

Diane Nesselhuf

Overview

In this day and age it can be very difficult to parent an adolescent. There can be a lot of societal obstacles in the way. Examples of these obstacles include drugs, sexually transmitted diseases, violence, and peer pressure. There are also numerous family pressures—divorce, parents' careers, blended families—which intertwine with these parenting challenges.

Most materials dealing with parent and adolescent relationships start with communication. This is important, but counselors need to back up and just look at development, not only the adolescent's development, but the parent's development as well. Since professional school counselors are developmental specialists, who better to help the students and families understand about the dynamics and conflicts of dealing with developmental changes?

Most parents of adolescents are between the ages of 35 and 60, a period we refer to as middlescence.

What is happening in these middle years to parents, and how does this affect their parenting? What is happening in these adolescent years and how does this impact the relationship with their parents?

Everyone in a family is going through a developmental stage. It does not matter what the family makeup is. When working with families, it is sometimes helpful to briefly discuss development and explain that it is a never-ending process.

Middlescence is a time when parents themselves are meeting many challenges. What is the family system? How has it changed? There are numerous societal and economic pressures placed on parents. They are probably re-evaluating their lives and careers. Sometimes there is a feeling of restlessness or discontent. Is this all I'm going to achieve in life? The middlescence's physical appearance and stamina have changed. They now see gray hair and wrinkles when they look in the mirror. People in this age group have to juggle career, family, and community involvement. They are sometimes called the "sandwich generation." They not only can have one or more adolescents, but they may have parents who now need care.

Instead of wondering what it means to be a woman or a man (one of the tasks of adolescence), the midlife individual becomes concerned about what it means to be a full human being. Going through their own identity crisis can leave parents too exhausted to want to deal with their children's emotional turmoil. As they question the choices that they have made, they can appear jaded and disgruntled just when their children need them to be optimistic and excited about their plans. The parents' opinions about their past may leave them overly opinionated about what is best for their children's future (McBride, 1987).

Just as any developmental stage has some negative experiences, (we'll call this growth experiences), there are also many positive things. Life can acquire a new and deeper meaning. Priorities are reordered and new directions pursued. Attitudes of understanding and tolerance toward others may be strengthened (Medinger & Varghese, 1981).

Adolescence, like middlescence, is a growth experience. Adolescents experience many physiological changes and these children come in all shapes and sizes with their variability of physical development. They have emotional swings, which they don't understand. They are establishing personal and career goals for themselves, consciously or subconsciously. They are struggling with their identity. Who are they and where do they fit in? They are self centered and think that everyone is looking at them. They can be restless, discontented, and confused. They can be argumentative. This is a new function of their cognitive ability. Amidst all this are the pressures of society, the family, school, and their peers. It is a time when they see things as black and white and they are struggling to find the gray areas.

Adolescents know their job is to eventually leave home, so they must individuate, which takes enormous amounts of energy. The teen is trying to break free right when the parents see their days as parents coming to an end, so they have a tendency to control more.

In comparing adolescent and middlescent development one can now see how and why there are conflicts.

- Both are dealing with physical changes.
- Both can be struggling with identity.
- Both can be restless, confused, and discontented.
- Both can be setting personal and career goals.

The comparison goes on and on. Parents and teens need to identify their similarities and differences and discover why there may be conflicts. An example of this is the mother getting upset when her teenage daughter spends an enormous amount of time in front of the mirror. Could some of this annoyance be that the mother is dealing with her own changes in her physical appearance?

After parents have some understanding of development, the counselor can then proceed to work with the parent on parenting styles and communication techniques.

There are numerous parenting styles: controlling, relationship, permissive, democratic, inconsistent, combinations, and many others. Most parents need to understand how they parent and how the adolescent reacts to their parenting. The counselor should be knowledgeable in the parenting styles and help the parents develop one that fits their beliefs and allows the teen to meet his/her individuation needs. The parent and teen need to have clear boundaries. What is the parent's responsibility in this family? What are the teen's responsibilities? What are shared responsibilities? They also need to discuss what the parents believe are negotiable and non-negotiable items. Examples of nonnegotiable items might be no drug use and car safety. Examples of negotiable items might be curfew and chores around the house. As an adolescent grows older, rules can change to agreements. Agreements give the teen some ownership and more responsibility.

When dealing with students, the counselor can help them understand their parent's-guardian's needs and development, and the conflicts that occur.

The discussion of life-long development and conflicts can be utilized in group settings, family sessions, parenting classes, peer helping, and in many other situations.

Parenting teens can be the most challenging and rewarding part of parenthood. In order for this to take place, parents must first understand about themselves, their teen, and then realize that parenting an adolescent differs from parenting a child. The following are some guidelines for helping parents survive and enjoy life with their adolescent.

- Don't do for your teen what they can do for themselves.
- It works better to have agreements rather than rules.
- Never say, "these are the best years of your life."

- Always ask yourself, "Is this meeting my needs, or my teen's?"
- Remember—mistakes are opportunities to learn.
- You are not the only parent going through whatever problem it is—you and your teen will survive.
- Your job as a parent, is not to improve your teenager, but to improve your relationship with your teen.
- Be sure your happiness is not based on your teen's success.
- You don't have control—you have influence.
- Model the behavior you expect.

References

Kirshenbaum, M., & Foster, C. (1991). *Parent teen breakthrough.* New York, NY: Plume.

McBride, A. B. (1987). *How to enjoy a good life with your teenager.* Tuscon, AZ: Fisher Books, 49.

Medinger, F., & Varghese, R. (1981). Psychological growth and the impact of stress in middle age. *International Journal of Aging and Human Development, (Vol.13,* 247-63.

Nelson, J., & Lott, L. (1991). *I'm on your side.* Rocklin, CA: Prima Publishing.

Pipher, M. (1994). *Reviving Ophelia.* New York, NY: Ballantine Books.

Diane Nesselhuf, NCC, NCSC is a professional school counselor at East High in Sioux City, Iowa.

11

Keys To Leading Successful School Groups

Teesue H. Fields & Rosemarie Smead

Overview

Many school counselors now use both counseling and psychoeducational groups as a routine part of their school counseling program. Here are some key components that will help school counselors maximize the success of their school groups.

Fitting the Treatment to the Problem

Group is more than just individual counseling with larger numbers. It is a medium based on behavioral modeling and interpersonal support theories which provide an opportunity for students to try new behaviors. The group should act as a support as members explore their own lives and learn new skills. If the counselor can only do two or three groups a year, it is better to use group work for those kinds of problems where group can be most powerful. If the primary intent is to teach new skills, the counselor should first ask if this could be done in classroom guidance, thus helping many more students. If the primary intent is to change problem behavior, the counselor must consider whether the student first needs individual counseling. Group work should be used when the counselor is convinced that group is the most effective way to deal with a particular topic or problem.

Selecting Group Members

Once a school counselor has decided that group work is the most appropriate treatment choice, then the next key is selection of the group members. Gazda (1989) maintained that fifty percent of a group's success could be accounted for by the appropriate selection of members. Interviewing the prospective group members allows the counselor time to get to know the students, explain group purpose and norms, and get informed assent from the student. A thorough interview sets clear expectations and facilitates the establishment of group norms.

When selecting students, it is important to achieve balance along several dimensions. Smead (1995) asserts that having members who are homogeneous in some aspects and heterogeneous in other aspects allows there to be enough differences for modeling new behaviors and enough similarities to develop cohesion and universality. Through balancing roles of group members, the group can include students who differ with regard to skills, attitude, and stages of the common problem.

The important outcome is a group that can function well together and form a cohesive, supportive whole. While this may mean excluding some students whom teachers or administrators want in the group, it is important for the counselor to consider the needs of the group above those of individual members.

Giving the Sessions a Framework

The amount of time for group counseling is usually very limited in schools. By using a clear framework, the group maximizes the time available and the students know what to expect. Corey and Corey (1992) report that structure can help to build group norms and encourage positive interactions. If this is a psychoeducational group, the session might start with either an icebreaker or a focusing activity on the day's topic. Group members may share and discuss the topic, voice ideas for application, and, finally, have a processing time. A counseling group might also use an opening activity, but it is more likely to begin by checking on the status of students' feelings or by examining members accomplished goals from the previous week. The counselor might use a specific technique to move the group onto a new level (such as a role play), followed by the group working on individual concerns and goals. The counseling group also ends with a processing time. It is up to the leader to move the session from section to section so that each part gets sufficient time.

Building Trust and Cohesion

Group should be a place where students feel free to share their concerns and where they can risk new behaviors. This will only be possible if the students trust each other. Typically, the first two or three sessions of group include a focus on trust building and trust testing. In each session members can be given the opportunity to share personal information or feelings, starting with information that is non-threatening (such as hobbies) and proceeding gradually to deeper levels of disclosure (e.g. the thing that makes you most afraid). If the group has a common problem then the self disclosure can be on topics related to the problem, but the problems are still processed from the general (what are the hardest things about a divorce) to the specific (how does the divorce affect you). In this way everyone in the group gradually takes some risks and gradually builds trust.

Cohesion in a group builds slowly. Ultimately, the leader wants the group members to take pride in the successes of other members and be supportive of their failures. When the members feel that what effects one individual effects the group, then cohesion is happening. The leader can facilitate cohesion by having students share in a joint project, by having students make supportive statements to each other and by encouraging other group skills, such as linking and connecting.

Linking and Connecting

The power of the group is in the relationship among the members. Since groups in schools are time-limited, the leader must use linking and connecting skills early and often to facilitate the multiple relationships involved. This skill uses a simple formula to teach students to notice thoughts, feelings, and behaviors they have in common, and to share this information with the other student(s), and get feedback from that student regarding how they experienced the connection. "Jeremy, I felt connected (or linked) to you when you said your grandma died. My grandpa died and I really felt crummy like you did." By consistently encouraging, modeling, and reinforcing linking statements among members, the leader quickly teaches the students to break the habit of unilateral communication with the leader and establish connections with each other. Other linking statements or questions could be: "What other kinds of feelings do you have when this happens," or "Who else has ever felt like this." When the leader encourages linking early in the group, it maximizes the opportunity for realizing the group goals.

Processing

Processing involves asking open-ended questions at the end of each group that allows students to process what they have experienced in group that day. Processing reminds students that what they do in group is an opportunity to change feelings and behavior and then take these changes to the world outside group.

According to Smead (1995) processing involves four levels of questions: intrapersonal (what went on inside you today), interpersonal (what happened in the group), new thoughts, feelings, or behaviors (what did you learn), and application of new knowledge (how will you apply what you've learned). By using various questions to tap the four levels, the counselor allows the students to pull together what they have learned. Processing also contributes to group cohesion and encourages linking and connecting by asking what members learned from each other.

Conclusion

In using group work, school counselors have a powerful treatment tool that can effect the lives of more students than can be served through individual counseling. The school counselor who uses appropriate selection, trust building, a framework for each session, linking, and processing has the greatest chance to lead a successful group.

References

Corey, M.S., & Corey, G. (1992) *Groups: Process and practice* (4th ed.). Pacific Grove: Brooks/Cole.

Gazda, G.M. (1989). *Group counseling: A developmental approach* (4th ed.). Boston: Allyn & Bacon.

Smead, R. (1995). skills and techniques for group work with children and adolescents. Champaign, IL: Research Press.

Teesue H. Fields, Ed.D. is assistant professor and Rosemarie Smead, Ed.D. is professor and coordinator of Counselor Education at Indiana University Southeast, New Albany, Indiana.

Program and
Policy
Development

12

School Counselor As Change Agent in Education Reform

Carolyn B. Sheldon

Overview

Education is being challenged by the constant and ever expanding presence of innovation and reform. It is unrealistic, however, to expect reform to take place in a system like education, which is not organized to engage in change. If our educational system became a learning organization, dealing with change would be a normal part of work, not just a response to the latest reform. School counselors can be agents of that change by forming partnerships with school staff and by learning about and understanding the complexities of the change process.

Discussing Change

What are the components of change that educators need to examine so as to create a positive culture for change?

Examining the pressures to change: Counselors can help staff and others gain insights and understanding about change and its personal and professional impact on each of us. Everyone has witnessed many major changes within society in their lifetime. In a brief reflection of these changes, counselors can confirm the following as important insights about change: *CHANGE* is a process; it happens in time. *TRANSITION* is a psychological reorientation to a change. *CHANGE* is accomplished by individuals first, then institutions. *CHANGE* is a highly personal experience. *INDIVIDUALS CHANGE* at different rates in different ways.

In reflecting on the major changes in education within the last five years one can readily identify several key changes that have impacted educators' positions and have caused a spectrum of emotional responses, ranging from anxiety to fulfillment. For example, education has moved from individual subjects to integrated instruction, from pencil and paper to word processing, and from competitive learning to cooperative learning. Everyone must learn to manage change. *CHANGE* is inevitable; it is disturbing when done to us, exhilarating when done by us and brings opportunity when one plans and gets ready for it. Staying ahead of change requires anticipating what is going to have to be done and then doing it while there is still time to exercise choice and influence events. Counselors can help school staff and parents be a vital part of change process.

Transition Stages for Individuals

In exploring how change impacts us as individuals, researchers often define the path of people in change and transition as made up of four phases: Denial, Resistance, Exploration, and Commitment. Scott and Jaffe define the Transitional Curve using the Chinese character for crisis which consists of two parts: one signifies danger, and the other opportunity (1989b). Flora/Elkind Associates add the concept that we feel danger when in denial and resistance phases and opportunity when in the exploration and commitment phase.

To help people move out of the first three stages of change and to celebrate refocusing, counselors can facilitate the identification of useful strategies such as those mentioned below (Scott & Jaffe, 1989b).

During Denial
- Give individuals information
- Confirm that the change will take place
- Share the reason for the change
- Explain what to expect and suggest actions they can take to adjust
- Talk to people in person
- Share your own feelings

During Refocusing/Collaboration
- Set long-term goals
- Concentrate on team building
- Create a mission statement
- Validate those responding to the change; reward small accomplishments
- Provide the big picture; explain why and offer a step-by-step plan
- Model new behaviors
- Celebrate successes

During Resistance
- Listen and acknowledge feelings
- Respond empathetically
- Don't try to talk people out of their feelings or tell them to change
- Let them vent and don't take it personally; relate changes to the system
- If possible, protect people from further changes that can wait

During Exploration/Management of Change
- Focus on priorities
- Provide any needed training
- Follow up on projects underway
- Set short-term goals; try new ideas on a small scale
- Conduct brainstorming, vision and planning sessions
- Help people prioritize

Fear of Loss: People Do Not Fear Change, They Fear Loss

The most common error in making change is to underestimate the effect it has on people, including feelings of loss. In discussing the potential losses resulting from change in an education setting, counselors can refer to Scott and Jaffe, and to Bridges' outline of potential losses resulting from change:

Relationships: Loss of co-workers, students, supervisors, communities

Turf: Loss of physical space, assignment, organizational power and influence, responsibilities

Structure: Roles, routines, policies, procedures

Competence: Knowledge, skills, and abilities

Sense of Direction: Purpose and meaning, what is to be done and why

Security: Expectations about the future, sense of control, predictability

Helping People During Change:

Here are some basic tips that are repeated in many, many sources:
- Give as much information as possible. Repeat as often as necessary.
- Tell the truth. Nobody has all the answers. If you don't know an answer, say so.
- Accept the feelings of others. Don't tell people how they

should feel.
- Be careful not to engage in self-fulfilling prophecies like "that won't work." We don't know yet what will work.
- Follow up questions, rumors, or concerns. Get the facts.
- Ask for information that may be helpful to the change project.
- Listen, Listen, Listen

Stages in Group Transition:
Like individuals, groups pass through stages during a change process. An often used description of stages of group development identifies moving from forming to storming, to norming to performing. Within each stage the group confronts major issues as follows:

Forming: expectations, purpose, belonging
Storming: power, relevance, conflict
Norming: roles, tasks, outcomes
Performing: performance, results, endings, celebrations (Scott & Jaffe, 1989a)

During the process of development, counselors help staff and parents see that the group willingness to change can be high initially but may slide during the storming phase and pick up again during the last two phases. It is noted, however, that the group's ability to deal with change, the group's competence, usually shows a steady upward learning curve.

Making complex change happen within a group requires five key elements: Vision, Skill, Incentives, Resources, and Action Plan. If all elements are present, change can occur. If any element is missing, the end product will not be changed. It could result in confusion, anxiety, gradual change, frustration or false starts.

In the following statements taken from many sources, counselors can identify key understandings about change.

Learnings about change:
- Change takes time and persistence.
- Individuals go through stages in the change process and it entails developmental growth in feelings and skills.
- Change strategies are most effective when they are chosen to meet people's needs.
- Change is made by individuals first, then institutions.
- Administrative support and approval is needed for change to occur.
- Developing a critical mass of support is just as important as

developing administrative support.
- An individual or committee must take responsibility for organizing and managing the change.
- The objective is to benefit students, not just "convert" staff.
- Successful change is planned and managed.

Recommended Course of Action

Changes in the role for counselors must keep pace with changes in education reform. Counselors can be part of leadership teams that provide technical and staff support in the school so that change efforts do not flounder. Helping staff relax into productive change, by explaining each step of the process, is far more productive than having them stiffen themselves against the winds of change. Facilitators are critical components of successful reform efforts. Counselors are trained facilitators.

After creating a positive culture for change, counselors can help staff, parents, site councils, etc., take the next steps in developing group process skills. New behaviors must be learned and team building extended to the entire school and beyond. Process and content are interrelated. Finding time for learning group process skills enhances prospects for success. Counselors can be the skilled change agents pushing for changes around them, helping to form teams necessary to bring about continuous improvements.

References

Bridges, W. (1991). *Managing organizational transitions.* Menlo Park, CA.: Addison-Wesley Publishing Co., Inc.

Flora/Elkind Associates. *Changes programs, managing the human side of change.* San Francisco.

Perry, N.S. (1992). *Educational reform and the school counselor.* Ann Arbor, MI: ERIC Clearinghouse on Counseling and Personnel Services. (ERIC Document Reproduction Service No. 347 491.)

Scott, C. D., & Jaffe, D. T. (1989a). *Managing organizational change.* Menlo Park, CA: Crisp Publications, Inc.

Scott, C. D., & Jaffe, D. T. (1989b). *Managing personal change.* Menlo Park, CA: Crisp Publications, Inc.

Carolyn B. Sheldon is the Assistant Director of Student Services, Portland Public Schools, Portland, Oregon and Past President of the American School Counselor Association, 1995-96.

13

School-to-Work Programs and the School Counselor

Judith M. Ettinger & Nancy Perry

Overview

Nearly a century has passed since Parsons emphasized the importance of helping young people transition from school to work. Today the focus of these efforts is on a comprehensive school-to-work program that requires a dynamic career development component for all students. Counselors provide leadership for this component by designing and delivering a program that includes developmentally appropriate experiences and activities which are designed to promote career awareness and career exploration for all students. The program is not the sole responsibility of the counselor, however. All educators, parents, and community leaders need to be involved in the career development component of a school-to-work program.

The Issues

The School-to-Work Opportunities Act was written as a response to profound changes taking place in the world of work. School-to-Work transition legislation clearly states the strong need for career development programs for all students. Students will need to do career planning and they will need to be aware of the many options available to them. This means information sharing; outreach; communication; providing exposure to formal and informal experiences that promote career development; understanding and communicating trends in career and labor market information to students, parents, and other educators; job placement; work experience programs; counseling and assessment; and public relations. The guidance and career development support services that are part of a school-to-work program are not separate or different from the rest of the work that a counselor does. Counselors have always provided leadership in career development programs, including initiatives and programs such as college prep,

Tech Prep, cooperative education, career academies, and work experience programs. To continue as effective leaders, counselors' knowledge of initiatives connected with school-to-work programs must be kept current. This chapter summarizes the career development language in the school-to-work legislation and, in particular, highlights the role of the counselor in these programs.

The Role of the Counselor

Before moving into the content of the legislation, it is important to focus first on the role that counselors are expected to play. First, they should provide leadership in developing school programs that provide formal and informal experiences to promote career development for all students. Examples of the kinds of activities that might meet this role would include designing a comprehensive K-12 career development program that is developmentally appropriate, designing and delivering a job shadowing program for juniors and seniors, establishing a speakers' bureau so that students have access to information about careers in their community, or overseeing a career portfolio program in the middle and high school.

Second, counselors should be informed about the curricular options in their school and about the career and labor market profiles in their community. This means that counselors need to have current information on workforce trends, legislative initiatives (both federal and state), and programs that can successfully help students transition from school to work. Examples are maintaining information about the school's Tech Prep program, understanding the kinds of decisions that need to be made for a particular student to succeed in a youth apprenticeship program, knowing which jobs will be in demand in the coming decade, and knowing where students can find information about a particular occupation (e.g., wage rates, types of industries where jobs are plentiful, job outlook, education and training needed to enter a particular occupation).

The third role is to communicate and market that information to students, parents, other school staff, and community members. This is a difficult process but critical if others are to understand the vast knowledge that is available to help students make informed decisions about, and prepare for, a variety of career options.

The fourth role is to develop partnerships and cooperative relationships, which can be either formal or informal between two or more parties who are charged with the common goal of easing school to-work transitions. A well-planned partnership is a benefit in a number of ways. Each partner knows that his or her work is reinforced and supported by others. Partnerships eliminate duplication of services and send a clear message to the community that facilitating school-to-work transition requires educational reform which must be the responsibility and commitment of everyone. As a result of success in these four roles, students will be served with higher quality programs.

Career Development Language in School-to-Work Legislation

The career development language in school-to-work legislation encourages schools to help all students seek a career path in which they can succeed, by assisting them in understanding and processing information and knowledge as they proceed along their chosen path.

School-to-Work initiatives are written into the legislation in two ways: the Perkins Act in Title IIIE (Tech Prep) and the School-to-Work Opportunities Act of 1994 (STWOA). Tech Prep programs must contain seven elements: an articulation agreement, appropriate curriculum development, teacher training, counselor training, equal access for special populations, and preparatory services. Although career development is implied in all components, it is explicitly mentioned in four of the seven components. Component 2, Appropriate Structure speaks to curriculum development. Included with this component is the notion of curriculum maps and career majors. These are the career pathways that students, teachers, and parents not only need to understand but need to know enough about to make a reasonable decision concerning the curriculum and career path they wish to pursue. Component 5, counselor training, recognizes the critical role of counselors in the Tech Prep plan. A successful program depends on a comprehensive developmental guidance program that affects the individual's attitude toward learning, education, identification of career goals, and determination of the means to reach those goals. Students need exposure to multiple opportunities over a period of time to assess self, the world of work, and to set realistic goals. Counselors also play a critical role in components 6 and 7, equal access for special populations and preparatory services, which can include outreach and recruitment, career and personal counseling, and vocational assessment and testing, among other activities.

The STWOA requires core components and goals but does not cite a single strategy for fulfilling those requirements. They can be met, for example, by a Tech Prep program that adds a work experience component, career academies, apprenticeship programs, or business education compacts. The legislation does require all programs to have three components, all of which contain a strong career development component: work-based learning, school-based learning, and connecting activities.

The work-based component involves counselors in planning job training and work experiences, in work place mentoring, and in ensuring instruction in workplace competencies and a variety of industry elements. Although it is unrealistic for counselors to take sole responsibility for this component, they should be involved in the planning and dissemination of information about this component.

The school-based component includes career exploration and counseling activities, identification of a career major, engagement in an academic and vocational program that meets requirements needed to earn a skills certificate, and regularly scheduled student evaluations to assess progress.

The component that sets this legislation apart from other legislation is the connecting activities. This component includes coordination of work-based learning opportunities between student and employers; serving as a liaison between students, parents, teachers, school administrators and employers; training for teachers and school site mentors; matching students with work-based learning opportunities; and providing technical assistance in designing work-based learning opportunities. The counselor cannot be expected to perform all of these tasks but should be involved in the process.

Another critical component of the legislation which needs to receive attention from counselors is the concept of "career major." According to the legislation, it is a coherent set of courses that prepare students for a first job by training them for work in broad occupational clusters. It typically includes at least two years of secondary schooling and one or two years of postsecondary school and leads to a high school diploma, skills certificate, and a one or two year postsecondary certificate or degree which may lead to further training.

Within all these components of the legislation, counselors need to assume the role previously described, in order to establish an effective program: providing experiences that promote career development, staying informed, communicating labor market information, and establishing formal and informal partnerships.

Strategies That Meet Career Guidance Needs
Within School-to-Work Initiatives

Effective strategies include:

- establishment of a comprehensive career guidance program structured around competencies, and indicators as standards that define what needs to be learned or achieved through participation in the program,
- classroom activities which address career development competencies and indicators within the classroom through team work between counselors and teachers, or by the teacher using a career development activity to teach a curriculum concept in courses such as language arts, science, math, and social studies,
- portfolios that are designed to guide students through the career development process by establishing a personalized, sequential career planning journal type of product, and
- learning experiences that are based on, and in, some type of work setting or simulated work setting such as school-based enterprises, job simulation labs, class projects, mock business projects, community service learning or school-linked summer employment.

Conclusion

The counselor, as the leader of career development initiatives in the school, is being asked to respond in new ways to assist students in preparing for their futures. Supportive legislation such as the School-to-Work Opportunities Act is the federal government's response to major challenges faced by schools, which are educating students for success in the 21st century. Those who authored the legislation believe that when young people leave school unequipped to perform in the workplace, everyone loses. This legislation will spur the creation of well-marked paths students can follow as they move from school to higher education, or to their first jobs. There are many approaches for implementing the legislation. Whatever route is taken, the career development component, with the counselor in the leadership position, is an important element which ensures that students not only receive academic and vocational skills, but also helps them participate in activities and classes which are designed to enhance the career decision-making of all students.

References

Ettinger, J. (1995). *Improving career counseling services*. Madison, WI: University of Wisconsin, School of Education, Center on Education and Work.

Facilitator's Manual, Get A Life: Your Personal Planning Portfolio for Career Development. American School Counselor Association

Lester, J. N. (Ed.). (1992). *From pilot to practice: Strengthening career development programs*. Washington, DC: National Occupational Information Coordinating Committee.

Paris, K. A. (1994). *Planning and implementing change for school-to-work transition*. Madison, WI: University of Wisconsin, School of Education, Center on Education and Work.

Pauly, E., Kopp, H., & Haimson, J. (1994). *Home-grown lessons: Innovative programs linking work and high school*. New York, NY: Manpower Demonstration Research Corporation.

Judith M. Ettinger, Ph.D. is a Senior Staff Member at the Center on Education and Work at the University of Wisconsin-Madison.

Nancy Perry, NCC, NCSC, is a Career Development Specialist at the National Occupational Information Coordinating Committee (NOICC) in Washington, D.C.

Career Development and the School Counselor

Linda L. Kobylarz

Overview

The kinds of knowledge, skills, and experiences students need to perform competently in the workplace of the 21st century are changing. The emergence of intensely competitive global markets, companies down-sizing and restructuring for high productivity, and the rapid acceleration of technological change are but a few of the factors impacting today's workplace and workers. Employers seek workers who not only have technical skills, but, equally as important, they desire workers who have an array of workplace know-how skills. In addition to the basics (strong communication and math skills), successful workers in the high performance workplace need critical thinking skills. They are also expected to display individual responsibility, sociability, integrity and honesty, positive self-esteem, and self-management skills. Workers must be prepared to use resources and technology productively; demonstrate positive interpersonal skills; use a variety of informational skills; and understand social, organizational, and technological systems (Secretary's Commission on Achieving Necessary Skills, 1991). Our students will be confronted with continued and dramatic change in the workplace; we are faced with the challenge of preparing them for that workplace.

Since the early 1980s numerous studies have been undertaken to ascertain the state of American education. One message from these studies is that education has failed to keep pace with the types of knowledge and skill requirements needed in the new workplace. The reports call for a revised curriculum that is both more relevant and more rigorous for all students. We must become a nation of lifelong learners and each of us must learn to manage our careers in a workplace where most workers will change their jobs ten or eleven times over their lifetime (U.S. Department of Education, 1991). It is clear that the career development of each of our citizens will affect the ability of our country to compete globally and maintain our high quality of life.

The School-to-Work Opportunities Act (STWOA) of 1994 represents a new education and career development strategy that provides all students with a foundation for lifelong learning that will help them compete in our turbulent world. Successful school-to-work transition requires a joint effort involving the education system, the home/family structure, business/industry, and a wide variety of community agencies and organizations. The School-to-Work Opportunities Act recognizes that comprehensive career development programs, designed to help individuals make and implement informed educational and occupational choices, are essential to the success of the school-to-work process. An appreciation for the role of career guidance and counseling is indicated throughout the Act.

Career Development is Key

As schools restructure to better meet the needs of student, business, and community stakeholders, the importance of career development cannot be overemphasized. What does career development encompass? Super (1976) defined career as "the sequence of occupations and other life roles which combine to express one's commitment to work in his or her total pattern of self-development." It follows then that career development is the process by which we develop and refine our self-identity as it relates to many life-and-work roles. It is a lifelong process that weaves through the tapestry of our total lifestyle — work, education, family, social, civic, and leisure.

In the mid-1980s, the National Occupational Information Coordinating Committee (NOICC) launched the National Career Development Guidelines project as a major, nationwide effort to foster excellence in career development for people of all ages, genders, and cultural backgrounds. The Guidelines are the result of a collaborative effort among NOICC, State Occupational Information Coordinating Committees (SOICCs), and leading career counseling and development professional organizations. The Guidelines offer helpful direction to schools that seek to establish a comprehensive career development program:

1. They provide a blueprint of career development competencies that children, youth, and adults should master and they identify standards or indicators of evidence that demonstrate that individuals have attained

those competencies. The career development competencies are grouped into three categories—self-knowledge, educational and occupational exploration, and career planning.
2. They offer information about the structure, support, and commitment necessary in schools that desire to implement effective career development programs.
3. They outline the competencies needed by counselors to deliver high quality programs (NOICC, 1996).

The School Counselor's Role in Career Development

School counselors should provide leadership and management of career development programs. The American School Counselor Association (ASCA) policy statement on career guidance explains that:

> The school counselor's role covers many areas within a school setting and career guidance is one of the counselor's most important contributions to a student's lifelong development. The school counselor, as a career guidance professional, is the person to assume leadership in the implementation of career development outcomes. Furthermore, indirect services to parents, staff and the greater community, as they relate to the career development outcomes for students, are also the counselor's responsibility. Indirect services include but are not limited to staff development, parent and school board presentation and the establishment of strong supportive linkages with business, industry and labor (ASCA, 1984).

ASCA further suggests that counselors take advantage of and utilize a wide variety of community resources and involve, to the greatest possible extent, all professional educators in the delivery of career guidance.

In order to fulfill this leadership role, school counselors may need to broaden their own expertise and sphere of activity. Drawing on the competencies created by the National Career Development Association, *The National Career Development Guidelines Handbook* outlines competencies for counselors who design and deliver career development programs. The competencies are grouped into seven major areas: *counseling, information, individual and group assessment, management and administration, implementation, consultation, and special populations.* School counselors are seen as proactive program designers, coordinators, managers, and evaluators of career development programs that reach all students from kindergarten through high school and beyond.

Career Development Programs

Career development programs reflect the sequential nature of the career development process. The focus of activities for K-6 is awareness, 7-8 investigation, 9-10 exploration, and 11-12 preparation for entry-level employment or advanced preparation. At each level the program has specific goals and is structured to include *all* students. In addition, the career development program:

- Is identifiable but integrated with other programs within the school.
- Enhances the career development knowledge, skills, and abilities of all students by establishing program standards.
- Uses coordinated activities designed to support student achievement of the standards.
- Supports the delivery of services through qualified leadership; diversified staffing; adequate facilities, materials, and financial resources; and effective management.
- Is accountable, with evaluation that is based on program effectiveness in promoting student achievement of the career development standards (NOICC, 1996).

School counselors typically use the intervention strategies of career guidance, career counseling, and career education to deliver career development programming. Career guidance uses a systemic approach to provide an organized series of experiences and information to students that help them master career development competencies. The scope and sequence of the guidance curriculum are determined by the counselor. The activities are usually delivered by a counselor to class-sized groups of students. In schools where there is a Teacher Advisor Program, selected aspects of the career guidance curriculum may be delivered by teachers under the direction of a counselor. Many schools have a weekly guidance period for students.

Career counseling is the interaction and communication between an individual student or small group of students and a counselor. It provides opportunities for students to explore personal issues related to career development, reflect upon and personalize information they have received, and apply their learnings to the crafting of individual education and career plans.

Career education uses teaching methods through the classroom to deliver certain aspects of the career development program to students. Teachers coordinate with counselors to integrate career development concepts into the standard curriculum.

A Team Approach

Although school counselors take a leadership role in managing the local career development program, they cannot implement it single-handedly. Comprehensive career development programs involve teachers and other staff members, administrators, parents, employers, and the community. Some schools establish a career development committee to oversee program implementation. Many counselors are active members of the school-to-work transition committee, to which they bring an important perspective. They ensure that the work-based and school-based learning experiences are sound and that they include a strong foundation of career exploration and counseling so that students can make informed decisions. Linking career development activities to other school initiatives is a productive strategy. Drug-free schools, conflict resolution, character education, drop-out prevention, and gender equity efforts deal with self-esteem, interpersonal relations, decision-making, problem solving and many other competencies that are also part of career development.

Career Development Methods

School counselors employ a wide variety of methods in their career development programs. Listed below are some tactics that others have found helpful.

- Integrate career concepts in academic and vocational lesson plans taught by teachers.
- Include career development in your guidance curriculum.
- Establish a Teacher Advisor Program to help deliver the guidance curriculum.
- Conduct a career development needs assessment for students, staff, parents, etc.
- Serve as a consultant for teachers, administrators, parents, mentors, and employers.
- Get involved with school-to-work transition activities.
- Provide career counseling and support to students.

- Open a career resource center to provide current, accurate, and unbiased information about occupations, postsecondary education, and employment opportunities to all students.
- Facilitate student awareness of career development services through school bulletin boards, morning announcements, teacher announcements, information flyers to parents, etc.
- Use technology, such as a computer-assisted guidance system and the Internet, to make career information available to students, parents, staff, and the community.
- Conduct career assessments to help students understand their interests, skills, etc.
- Create a process for all students to complete a career portfolio.
- Ensure that all students have an ongoing individual education and career plan.
- Involve students with business and industry representatives through field trips, career fairs, class speakers, phone interviews, E-mail and the Internet, Brown Bag lunches at school, Junior Achievement, and mentorships.
- Engage students in work-based learning through classroom "jobs," school enterprises, service learning, job shadowing, internships, Cooperative Education, Tech Prep, Youth Apprenticeships, part-time jobs, and volunteerism opportunities.
- Provide post-high school placement and follow-up services to students.
- Engage in active and ongoing public relations for your career development program with students, teachers, administrators, staff members, Board members, parents, employers, and the community.

Conclusion

The dramatic changes occurring in the workplace of the 21st Century necessitate that each of us becomes the manager of our own career development. In thousands of schools across the country, counselors are assuming new leadership roles in the design and implementation of comprehensive career development programs that begin in kindergarten and continue through the school years. In these programs a team effort is used to ensure that all students have opportunities to master competencies in the areas of self-knowledge, educational and occupational exploration, and career planning. Armed with a strong foundation in career development, students will be better prepared to engage in lifelong learning and meet the challenges of the new workplace.

References

ASCA. (1984). *Role statement: The school counselor in career guidance: Expectations and responsibilities*. Alexandria, VA: Author.

NOICC. (1996). *The national career development guidelines handbook, k-adult*. Washington DC: Author.

The Secretary's Commission on Achieving Necessary Skills, U.S. Department of Labor. (1991). *What work requires of schools: A SCANS report for America 2000*. Washington, DC: U.S. Department of Labor.

Super, D. E. (1976). Career education and the meaning of work. In *Monographs on career education*. Washington, DC: U.S. Department of Education, Office of Career Education.

U.S. Department of Education. (1991). *America 2000: An education strategy*. Washington, DC: Author.

For more information about career development contact the following: the U.S. Department of Education, Office of Vocational and Adult Education (202) 205-5440, the National Occupational Information Coordinating Committee (202) 653-7680, National School-to-Work Learning & Information Center (800) 251-7236, the ERIC/Counseling and Student Services Clearinghouse (800) 414-9769, the National Center for Research in Vocational Education (800) 762-4093, the American Counseling Association (703) 823-9800, the American School Counselor Association (703) 683-2722, the American Vocational Association (703) 683-3111, and the National Career Development Association (703) 823-9800 ext. 309.

Linda L. Kobylarz is a career development consultant and President of Linda Kobylarz & Associates. She served as Life Career Development Specialist for the American School Counselor Association, 1993-1994.

15

Creating a Business Advisory Council for School Counselors

Pat Schwallie-Giddis & Jackie M. Allen

Overview

As the 21st century approaches, American society faces some fundamental challenges that will determine future productivity, the quality of life, and the ability to be competitive in the global marketplace. No group or segment of the population should be denied access to adequate preparation for the workforce.

President Bill Clinton proposed that all students select a career field by the 11th grade and the Congress passed the School-to-Work Opportunities Act in May 1994 to support that concept. The role of the school counselor in this process is vital.

In order to provide a comprehensive approach to this initiative, school counselors need to reach out to the business community. One of the key concepts to assist in this process is the establishment of a business advisory council. Once counselors acknowledge their need to reach out into the community and create a link with business and industry leaders, the process can begin.

Getting Started

Preparation for establishing a business advisory council starts with the formation of a core group of supporters which may include the local school principal, a steering committee, the school counselor, the superintendent or district staff, or the school counselor association leader. These supporters will vary depending on whether the advisory council will serve an individual school, a school district, or a professional organization.

To begin at a local school site, some key players should be brought together in the school setting as a steering committee to discuss the need, role and function of a business advisory council. First, it will be necessary to clarify what the expectations of the council will be. The council may serve as an advisory group only, act as as an agent to develop school-community partnerships, become directly active in curriculum and program development, and/or provide technical and financial support to the local school. Once the role is clear, the group will identify the businesses and industries that currently impact on the entire community and make a list of contacts. Usually one meeting is adequate for this activity. Two or three business people who are well known to the steering committee members can be asked to make some suggestions for names that may not be on the list. It is important to allow enough time to finalize the initial contacts and give businesses a chance to be represented on the council.

Next, identification of potential leaders should take place. Two or three possible candidates for temporary chairperson should be discussed, one of whom should be chosen by the steering committee. Once the temporary chairperson has agreed to serve, a letter on professional letterhead inviting other potential members to attend an orientation meeting should be sent out. The letter should explain the purpose of the meeting and offer the business representatives an opportunity to serve the education community. The steering committee will be helpful in preparing this letter as well as an agenda for the first meeting.

Initial Meetings

The initial meeting is very important. A working agenda should be prepared ahead of time. All members of the council need to feel included and should have ample time to introduce themselves and explain why they are interested in being part of the council. Part of the meeting should include a general overview of the background information on why the temporary chair, the steering committee, and the school felt that a busines advisory council was needed. The meeting should be kept to a specified time; business and community leaders are very busy people and their commitment of time and energy should be respected and valued.

A plan of action for the council can be formulated through discussion. It is important to agree on a tentative plan for the future and establish the next meeting date, time, and place before council members leave the first meeting. In order to make the experience more relevant, and to assist the council members to become acquainted with the scope of school-to-work transition, assignments such as the following may be given:

- Visit a school and their counselor to get a clearer picture of what they are currently doing to prepare students for the workforce.

- Talk to at least two or three students about what they feel that they need in order to be prepared to leave school and enter the workforce.
- Talk to people at their place of work to determine the level of interest and commitment to this business advisory council concept and the new school-to-work concept.

The second meeeting sets the tone for the ongoing work of the council. Again the mission of the council should be clarified. Selection of the chair should be made, either by confirming the position of the Acting Chair or by electing a new chair. The role of the staff member, if one will be working with the council, should be clarified. The council is now ready to begin dealing with real issues and determine a plan of action. Having the advisory council members report on the assignments from the first meeting forms a consensus of the educational and community needs and establishes a shared purpose. Minutes of each meeting should be kept and mailed out in a timely manner.

Benefits of an Advisory Council

The establishment of a business advisory council has many benefits for the school counselor and the school guidance and counseling program. School-to-work transitions require that the school develop a link between the school and the community for career education and work experience. Business partnerships, to promote the school-to-work transition, are very important for student success in the world of work. School counselors and teachers need advice and assistance from the business world in both program and curriculum preparation. Business and industry can provide career information and technical support for career and school-to-work programs. Economic support for special programs and student scholarships may be another benefit. Business advisory council members become invaluable assests to a school counseling program when they advocate for the important role that school counselors play in school-to-work transition.

The ASCA Model

The American School Counselor Association (ASCA) created their Business Advisory Council, known as the ASCA National Business Advisory Board, during the Spring of 1992. This Board has developed guidelines for operation, membership qualifications, and a specific plan of action. To date several significant tasks, which may serve as examples for other advisory councils, have been accomplished by this Board:

- advocacy for school counselors at the congressional level
- a position paper on the Emerging Role of the School Counselor
- advocacy for school counseling at other professional associations such as the National Association of Secondary Principals national conference
- Town Meeting presentations at the annual ASCA Conferences
- increase of the awareness of the role of the counselor for business and industry
- a booklet on "Students and Jobs-Counselors Role in the School-To-Work Opportunities Act of 1994"
- a national essay and scholarship program
- sponsorship of specific association activities related to the council's mission

Conclusion

School counselors must become instrumental in the establishment of ongoing relationships within the business community so as to share the responsibility for training and employment. School counselors should play a significant role, in conjunction with other educators, in the development of school-business partnerships in their community and should undertake collaborative and coordinating roles in school-to-work transition. The establishment of an advisory council will provide the natural link between the educational and business communities. As school counselors initiate advisory councils in their local school districts, they will find that business and industry will become valuable allies in preparing students for successful transiton into the world of work. The same successes can be realized if counseling associations at the local and state level also develop business advisory councils. As it has been stated many times, "It takes a whole village to raise a child."

References

ASCA National Business Advisory Council. (1994). Procedural guidelines. Unpublished handouts.

ASCA National Business Advisory Council. (1994). *Position statement on the emerging role of the school counselor.* Alexandria, VA: ASCA.

Hamilton, B. (1995). School counselors: Bridging the gap. *Enter Here TM News,* 5, 2.

Monderer, J. H., & Miller, C. G. (1988). Strategies for a successful guidance advisory committee. *The School Counselor,* 35, 229-233.

What is the School Counselor's Role? (1995). *NASSP NewsLeader,* 42, 9.

Pat Schwallie-Giddis is the Assistant Executive Director for Professional Development of the American Vocational Association.

Jackie M. Allen, an ASCA Past President, is a consultant with Allen Consulting Associates. Both authors have served as members of the ASCA National Business Advisory Board.

16

Developing a Crisis Management Plan

Jan Gallagher & Doris Rhea Coy

Overview

Why is a crisis management plan needed? A crisis can range from an accident to planned criminal acts of violence. In a recent North Carolina survey, 14% of the children indicated that they had carried a weapon to school in the past month. Statistics report that teen suicides number 5,000 per year for the 15-to 25-year-old age group. Clearly schools are not immune to violence because crises occur. School crises may take many forms; from one sudden, brutal incident, to a series of small incidents which culminate in a large serious problem. A school can wait for a crisis to occur and then respond unprepared, or it can develop a thorough prevention and intervention plan and be prepared to cope with the crisis when it occurs.

The Role of the School Counselor

Very often the school counselor is the "point person," the person who must take the lead in a crisis situation in a local school. What person has more knowledge of human behavior than the counselor? Skilled in working with people and trained in anticipating responses, counselors are well qualified to lead the Crisis Management Team. Most school counselors have had extensive training in one or more of the following areas:
- Recognizing suicidal signs
- Coping with grief
- Sudden death
- Critical illness
- Accidents, severe injuries
- Random acts of violence
- Terrorist activities
- Gang violence

Developing the Plan

The first step in crisis management is an open discussion on the need for a plan. In light of the statistics, the school cannot afford to ignore this need. The school counselor should organize a forum to include all the stakeholders, i.e., community members, business people, parents, teachers, and students. The school should take the leadership role in this initial stage. This forum might be the beginning of a planning committee which would work *together* to develop a crisis management plan.

A comprehensive safety audit can be very useful to a planning committee. For example, the State Board of Education in Texas has a model safe-schools checklist to assess a school's safety strengths and weaknesses. This checklist provides a good definition of a safe school. The checklist is made up of two parts:

- The first part is a self-assessment tool which schools may use to evaluate needs and formulate plans related to implementing a comprehensive safety plan, including emergency and/or crisis procedures.
- The second part of the checklist contains questionnaires for teachers, parents and students. Such an instrument can be helpful in making decisions about prevention, intervention, and follow-up strategies. Interviews and surveys of parents, teachers, students, and community members can provide valuable insights into the crisis management conditions at the school or district. Because potential conditions for crises in a school/district vary an audit can assist in determining which groups or individuals have the greatest concerns and why.

The committee charge would be to formulate a model for the various crises which could affect individual students, faculty, school, or community. Examples of topics which might be covered include suicide threats, car/bus accidents, gas leaks, bomb threats, and other acts of violence. Key persons, from which to solicit input, would be campus police, maintenance workers, food service employees, transportation drivers, teachers, coaches, administrators, students, parents, and, of course, school counselors.

Crisis Management Steps

What should be in a crisis plan? Should there be a school district plan? Should there be an individual campus plan for each school? The answers are probably yes to both latter questions. These questions must be carefully addressed. Perhaps the plan is really a series of actions addressing many different kinds of crises. There are some general recommended guidelines in any crisis which must be followed in a District Crisis Plan and modified for individual campus crisis plans.

1. Administrators (Superintendent, principal, or other designee) are notified
2. Facts are verified, first by the Superintendent , principal or designee
3. Crisis team is notified *as soon as possible*, by the Superintendent, principal or designee
4. Facts are reviewed, and the next steps are outlined. These may include:
   a. Estimate potential impact on students, staff, parents and others
   b. Determine written information for use with school, classrooms, and groups
   c. Coordinate outside resources
   d. Establish on-site resources
5. Designate one media contact person. This is the most crucial and important guideline. One person means no mixed messages are sent; *thus* none are received.
6. Establish a communications center or rather, a command post, from which all information flows in and out.
7. Establish a counseling center with counselors, nurses, social workers, and other outside resource professionals from community agencies or area hospitals.
8. Debrief on a regular basis.

The Crisis Management Team

The key to the entire organizational process is the Crisis Management Team. A district team might include: Superintendent, Chief of District Police, Health Services Coordinator, Pupil Services/Counseling Coordinator, Director of Maintenance, Transportation, Media Officer, Superintendent's Secretary, and others (as determined by the incident). What are the personal characteristics of these team members? How do they respond in an emergency? What is their general personality/type or makeup?

In general, Crisis Team members have:

1. The ability to think clearly and act quickly when under stress.
2. A thorough knowledge of the school, school district and

community.

3. Flexibility in thinking, and in acting.
4. The ability to anticipate reactions and expect consequences.
5. The ability and desire to work with others and be part of a team.
6. A broad focus on life, open to all options and sources of information or assistance
7. Skills in one or more particular area of expertise, such as counseling, clerical skills, health services, facilities, buildings, power supplies, etc.

Crisis Team Functions

The Crisis Team has several primary functions. First, the Team takes the leadership in developing the initial Crisis Management Plan; for it is they who will be implementing that plan. In other words, they help prepare and train their colleagues. The team acts as a public relations group and informs outside resources of the plan. They engage these outside resources as community support, if and when needed. An example might be working with the local mental health groups to insure that agency counselors or other mental health professionals would be on call to assist school personnel.

In stemming the tide of violence and in making the school safe in the process, it is important to keep the following precepts in mind:

- Proactive responses are superior to reactive responses.
- A crisis or a violent act can occur in any school, but such an incident may be more likely in some schools than others.
- A school crisis is a district and a community problem.

Finally, the Crisis Team must review, evaluate, and make necessary changes in the Plan after every situation. Be aware that even in the best of plans there is always room for improvement. Each time a crisis occurs the Team will learn something new, gain confidence, and solidify as a TEAM.

Conclusion

There is no guarantee that a school will avoid all crises, leaders must take precautions to minimize the impact of a situation.

Comprehensive planning, with extensive community and school involvement, helps to generate the best plan and thus create a safeguard. In a crisis situation, a call to 911 is not enough; it is only a beginning.

References

Crisis Management Task Force. (1991). *Crisis Management Manual.* San Antonio, TX.

Kadel, S., & Follman, J. (1993, March). *Reducing school violence.* Tallahassee, FL: South Eastern Regional Vision for Education (SERVE).

National School Safety Center. (1994, November). *Studies show quality of life for many youth is threatened.* Malibu, CA: Author.

Texas Education Agency. (1994, April). *Safe Texas schools: Policy initiatives and programs.* Austin, TX.

Watson, R. (1995, February). A guide to violence prevention. *Educational Leadership.* Alexandria, VA: ASCD.

Jan Gallagher is the coordinator of Guidance and Testing in the Harlandale Independent School District in San Antonio, Texas. She is currently serving as the Post Secondary/Supervisor Vice President of the American School Counselor Association.

Doris Rhea Coy is in private practice as a consultant to business, education, government, & industry and Past President of the American Counseling Association. She has also served as President of the American School Counselor Association.

17

Designing an Outcome Based School Counseling System and Program

Tommie R. Radd

Overview

As a result of the need for counseling programs to demonstrate student outcomes and program accountability, it is important that programs are designed proactively for success. This requires that guidance and counseling programs have a broader comprehensive, developmental, competency-based focus; a focus that applies guidance concepts and skills which are developed through the counseling program to the day-to-day happenings in schools. Expanding perceptions of guidance and counseling from a service or program into a system is the key. The guidance program components, such as guidance curriculum, small group counseling, and individual counseling, are *systematically* interrelated and are applied into the school *system*. The guidance curriculum needs to be expanded to a guidance *system* that is the *foundation* of the classroom and the school building.

A systems approach that is interactive, interrelated, interconnected, and congruent is the basis for a successful guidance and counseling program. An interactive system identifies those program components that affect each other, such as behavior and curriculum. For example, the success of the guidance curriculum is based on the daily interactions of adults with students. An interrelated system identifies those daily happenings, which include guidance and counseling skills and concepts. An interconnected system identifies how everything in the guidance program connects with the school program and the learning process. A congruent system identifies those programs, policies, and daily processes in the school that fit with the concepts and skills developed through the guidance program. A guidance systems approach is central to the daily success of the educational process for all students. Also, a systems approach identifies those components of the educational process that can sabotage counseling program results.

The following information outlines the necessary components of a comprehensive, developmental, competency-based guidance system and how it is the basis for a systematic, comprehensive guidance and counseling program. Goals, competencies, and outcomes are integral within each system and program component. They may be defined as follows:

Goal: Global statements which reflect purpose and philosophy and indicate the long-term outcomes in each general and specific area.

Competencies: Statements that reflect the desired proficiencies in each general and specific area. These proficiencies are observable, measurable, developmental, and provide the basis for moving toward the global goal.

Outcomes: Statements that indicate what you will see when the competency is met. These statements indicate if a transference has been made into life skills.

Comprehensive Observation/Evaluation is needed to demonstrate accountability and maintain an outcome based guidance system and program. This observation/evaluation process needs to be structured as an on-going and annual component of the guidance system and program.

The Place of the Foundation System in the Guidance & Counseling Program

An interactive, systematic, counseling program is built upon the developmental foundation system. All program components are consistently represented from elementary school through high school. Developmentally appropriate content and variations on the amount of designated time per component is the primary differentiation among counseling levels. All program components, elementary through high school, require goals, competencies, and outcomes in order to maintain an outcome-based counseling program. Components of the guidance and counseling program include the following:

(1) The Foundation System—40% of the counselor's time allocation,

(2) Counseling Groups—30% of the counselor's time allocation,

(3) Individual Counseling—10% of the counselor's time allocation. The remaining 20% of the counselor's time include items 4-8:

(4) Classroom Enrichment Units,

(5) Staff Involvement—Programs/Groups/Conferences,
(6) Family Involvement Programs/Groups/Conferences,
(7) Resource Development, and
(8) Professional Teams/Committees.

Consultation, cooperation, communication, coordination, collaboration, and facilitation are important within each component of the foundation system. Each aspect is also important in working with students, staff, families, and the community.

A Developmental Guidance System: The Foundation

The Foundation System includes six interactive components: behavior management; self-talk/self-pictures; student, staff, and family development and skills; and observation/evaluation. The Foundation System is a system because it incorporates an interactive plan for behavior, self-talk/self-pictures, and curriculum. Consistent implementation of all three—behavior, self-talk/self-pictures, and curriculum—create the foundation and environment for positive outcomes: staff development, family programs and observation/ evaluation also are components of the System.

Self-concept is developed by day-to-day interactions with students. It is important that all interactions with students support a healthy self-concept. This can be accomplished through implementation of a self-concept process throughout each component of the guidance foundation system.

Behavior Management Component

The Behavior Management Component allows behavior to become a part of the learning process for both students and staff. This component provides the framework for healthy interactions in which behavioral challenges become opportunities for greater understanding and growth.

Self-Talk/Self-Pictures Component

Self-Talk/Self-Pictures is the process that allows "what we say and believe" to be congruent with "what we think and feel." The internal thoughts and pictures that students hold need to be supportive of the positive life goals of the student. Selected self-talk/self-pictures can be used to support the positive behavior plan.

Curriculum Component

After the behavior and the self-talk/self- pictures plans are in place, the environment and the internal base is established for the System activity process. This activity process provides the information and experiences for the development of a student skill base. These skills are in the strands of Self, Other Awareness, Self-

Control, Decision Making/Problem Solving, Group Cooperation, and Career.

Staff Development Component

This component supports the development of skills and approaches which are most effective for professionals and their students. In staff development sessions and in classroom modeling, it is important to demonstrate and create experiences that support a personal and professional growth plan for staff.

Family Involvement Component

The Family Component has two primary emphases:

    (1) family feedback regarding application of student skills at home, and

    (2) family support and education.

The use of the information provided in the other components can be used in family education.

System Observation/Evaluation

The comprehensive Observation/Evaluation process for the System includes planned qualitative and quantitative approaches. *The focus is positive observation, not deficits.* Established goals, competencies, and outcomes are the basis for the observation/evaluation process. Information feedback from students, staff, and families needs to be included.

The System Organization Plan

The System needs to be organized with a plan in order for the comprehensive goals, competencies, and outcomes to be realized for students, staff, and families. The System organization in most cases would be coordinated by the guidance and counseling administrator, the director of curriculum, or a similar designee. Input from an advisory committee, which is representative of the school and community populations, can be helpful.

The building counselor in most cases would coordinate the System at the building level. An organizational team needs to be identified and the process for the System implementation needs to be decided and communicated within the school district. Consistent organization within the buildings of the district is recommended due to the curricular and comprehensive nature of the System and the increased transient nature of student populations. Counselor-Teacher Teams are organized at the beginning of the school year and are recommended for maximum System results.

Conclusion

The importance of designing education programs based on a guidance system foundation and the need to incorporate that system as the base of a proactive systematic guidance and counseling program has been documented. This design is integral for demonstrating program accountability and student outcomes.

References

Gysbers, N.C., & Henderson, P. (1994). *Developing and managing your school guidance program.* (2nd ed.) American Association for Counseling and Development: Alexandria, VA.

Myrick, Robert D. (1993). *Developmental guidance and counseling: A practical approach.* (2nd ed.). Minn. MN: Educational Media Corporation.

Radd, T.R. (1993). *The grow with guidance system manual.* (2nd ed.). Canton,OH: Grow With Guidance.

Radd, T. R. (1993). *The grow with guidance system levels 1-7.* (2nd ed.). Canton, OH: Grow With Guidance.

Radd, T. R. (1993). *The invitational teaching survey-Primary & intermediate.* (2nd ed.). Canton, OH: Grow With Guidance

Thompson, C. & Rudolph, L. (1992) Counseling Children, (3rd ed.). Pacific Grove, CA: Brooks/ Cole.

Tommie R. Radd, Ph.D., CRC, LPC, is an associate professor of counselor education at The University of Nebraska at Omaha in Omaha, Nebraska.

18

Implementing the Developmental Comprehensive School Counseling Program Model

Jim Lukach

Overview

Current trends and issues in education indicate the need to implement a comprehensive school counseling program model to help students develop their educational/academic, personal/social, and career/vocational strengths and to become responsible and productive citizens.

The developmental approach is planned, preventative, and proactive. It contrasts with the traditional guidance approach, which addresses the needs of only a few students and is reactive, crisis-oriented, unplanned, and focused upon information, scheduling, records, and noncounseling functions. The developmental program focuses on activities which help students acquire understanding and skills to pass successfully through developmental stages of life. Sequential planned activities are coordinated by school counselors and implemented by the entire school and community. Counselors, peers, administrators, parents, teachers, and business and community members all promote student development in four basic ways: counseling, curriculum, consultation, and enhancement activities. The curriculum identifies the competencies to be attained by all students, and presents structured activities to help them achieve competence. Continuous, systematic student planning links the four components into an interactive program to promote and monitor individual student competence.

The written plan is the approved guide for the delivery of the curriculum model. The plan should include the following:
  (a) a mission statement,
  (b) program philosophy,
  (c) program goals,
  (d) time lines,
  (e) student competencies,

(f) delivery systems,

(g) resources needed,

(h) program components,

(i) implementation plan, and

(j) evaluations, student competencies, and program outcomes.

There are other resources that must be taken into consideration:

Resources

Resources fall into several major categories; each program component activity calls for different levels of resources to be effective.

Facilities: The school counseling center or office is the center of the activity. Since the program is not limited to those components provided by the school counselor, other facilities within the district and community are essential.

Material Resources: Current curriculum materials should be available and developmentally appropriate for program component activities.

Fiscal Resources: Adequate budgets ensure that the program is effectively developed, implemented, managed, and evaluated. Annual district funding assurances will ensure program continuity without reliance upon special grants.

Advisory Council: At both the district and school level, the advisory council should advise, support, monitor, and promote the development and evaluation of the school counseling program and provide feedback to school, home, and community about the program.

Human Resources: Staffing patterns must clearly show the organizational relationships among all staff members and others directly involved in delivering the school counseling program to the students. A clear delineation of tasks and activities ensures realistic expectations and job descriptions.

Beginning the New While Working in the Old

The decision to implement a model counseling program requires three to five years of full transition. Collaboration is needed from the entire school community at each stage of the transition. This is the beginning of an exciting, dynamic process involving the entire school community. With any major systemwide change, you will encounter questions and resistance until all the stakeholders understand and appreciate the value of the change. The hardest work occurs before change is implemented. Becoming aware, understanding, making a change, developing support, retraining, experimenting, and brainstorming are essential to the change process.

A Step-By-Step Planning Guide

Introduce the Initiative:
1. gather ground support from the Superintendent of Schools, the Board of Education, and the community,
2. establish the "school counseling team,"
3. learn about the various program models,
4. broaden support and enhancement through professional development workshops.

Organize for Change:
1. assess the current program and resources by interviewing staff, students, parents, and service providers,
2. compare the current program with an established program model to determine "fit,"
3. conduct the needs assessment to identify students and to determine need,
4. analyze data results of needs assessment,
5. develop mission statement and rationale.

Design the Program:
1. reallocate the current resources and identify new resources needed,
2. prioritize the needs of your students,
3. establish student outcomes to address needs,
4. review results with staff,
5. outline your 3-5 year plan,
6. develop a comprehensive written plan,
7. present proposal and timeline to your Board of Education, and
8. broaden support base in the school and community.

Prepare for the Transition:
1. organize the Advisory Council,
2. present the written plan for adoption,
3. present plan to the staff,
4. develop parents' and students' orientation to the program,
5. conduct staff training,
6. develop Model K-12 units,
7. expand counseling curriculum, and
8. initiate new counseling delivery system.

Implement the Program:
1. establish the master calendar,
2. initiate the resources and referral directory for counselor/ parents/staff,
3. initiate a professional development program, and
4. provide in-service training to work in the old program while phasing in the new program.

Evaluate the Results:
1. continue the school counseling team as a resource and program evaluation group,
2. up-date staff evaluations to reflect enhanced roles,
3. initiate student outcome evaluations,
4. propose program revisions to meet changing needs,
5. adjust professional development program to meet new needs,
6. report regularly to Board of Education, and
7. continue on-going participation with districts or schools also implementing program models.

Conclusion

The needs assessment is conducted to find out what your program should be doing to meet the needs of your students. Some needs are clearly expressed or perceived by your school distict and your community. Other needs are more subtle, requiring the schools counseling team to draw conclusions based upon the data you collect. The district needs assessment is the foundation of the developmental comprehensive program model.

Writing the curriculum comes after having analyzed the results of the needs assessment. This assessment will help set priorities for the curriculum based on what parents, students, staff, and the community have identified as important.

The counseling curriculum should correlate with your district's curriculum model, infusing the curriculum, where possible, within existing subject areas. However, the counseling curriculum is an equally important curriculum. Formal adoption and placement of the counseling curriculum within the district's curriculum guide assures legitimacy and parity of this curriculum with academic subjects.

References

Carr, J. V., Haslip, J., & Randall, J. (1988). *New Hampshire guidance and counseling program handbook: A guide to an approved model for program development.* Plymouth, NH: Plymouth State College.

Myrich, R. D. (1987). *Developmental guidance and counseling: A practical approach.* Minneapolis, MN: Educational Media Corp.

Perry, N. S., & Schwallie-Giddis, P. (1993, March). The counselor and reform in tomorrow's schools. *Counseling and human development, 25* (7).

Runte, J., Mascari, B., & Lukach, J.(1992). *Charting the 21st century: The New Jersey developmental program model.* NJ: NJ School Counselor Association.

Starr, M. F., & Gybers, N. C. (1988). *Missouri comprehensive guidance: A model for program development and implementation.* Jefferson City, MO: Missouri Department of Elementary and Secondary Education.

Jim Lukach, NCC, NCSC, is a school counselor in the Matawan-Aberdeen Regional School District, Matawan, NJ.

Strategic Planning for School Counselors

Jan Olson & Jackie M. Allen

Overview

As school districts struggle with the demands of national education standards and America 2000 goals, a plan is needed to restructure or reform the existing organizations. The downsizing of the 90s requires all organizations to work smarter and faster. School reform does not succeed without careful and systematic short- and long-term planning. School counselors, as part of local school organizations, also are challenged by the need to not only maintain their positions but also to reform their counseling and guidance programs.

The school improvement movement has rapidly spread across the United States. The central question in school reform is: whether what we are doing should be done at all? If we continue to do what we are doing, what will our school system look like in five to ten years? Or maybe we should ask what should our school systems be about? Dr. Lawrence W. Lazotte, at the Iowa Effective Schools Conference, stated that public schools, "Must be about the business of school improvement or be non existent in the 21st century" (1995).

School reform has become a necessity, and planning for change is an integral part of school reform. Strategic planning is a process for managing change in both school improvement and in comprehensive school counseling program development. A school counselor can serve as an effective facilitator of the strategic planning process because of his/her background in human development and group dynamics.

Strategic Planning

Strategic planning is about change. Strategic planning for an organization is the "process" of creating a mutually shared vision and mission and the specific steps to be taken to obtain that vision. It begins by clarifying values or beliefs and developing a mission. Environmental scanning techniques collect data for the purpose of identifying critical issues and plans of action. A creative tension emerges between the current reality and the future needs.

Clearly, strategic planning is the process for managing change. It yields a product—a strategic plan—which is a blue print for action. A strategic plan may be a three-to five-year project. The mandatory components of a strategic plan are:

1. Belief statement
   - a formal expression of an institution's fundamental values
   - its ethical code and overriding convictions
2. Vision
   - a mutually shared picture of the future which may be evolving
   - the "where" we want to go
3. Mission statement
   - the purpose of the organization
   - the "why" we want to go there
4. Environmental scanning
   - External Scanning - gathering information about the social, economic, political, and technological environment
     Example: There is a new governor in the capitol.
   - Internal Scanning - gathering information about the organizational and personal membership
     Example: School counselors are intuitive, feeling professionals
5. Goal Setting
   - establish three to five goals
   - a dream with a time frame, - milestones we expect to reach before too long
6. Strategies
   - processes to achieve goals (i.e. staff development, study teams)
7. Action Plans
   - operationalization of the goals and strategies
   - who is responsible, methodology, time line, expenses, evaluation

When a strategic plan is completed it is very important that the plan be published and distributed. The distribution of the plan declares the intent to change and the direction in which that change will be proceeding.

Strategic Planning and Operational Planning

In order to remain vital, every organization and school counseling program must be successful at two types of planning: strategic and operational. Organizations must decide what are the right things to do (strategic) and how to do them right (operational). The differences between Strategic and Operational Planning include:

Strategic Planning	Operational Planning
1. Deals with the longer term-future	1. Deals with short term (One year or less)
2. Deals with growth and change	2. Deals with maintaining programs
3. Deals with whole system	3. Deals with parts
4. Driven by vision	4. Driven by budget

Using both types of planning, the organization moves forward with short-term and long-terms goals in place. The strategic planning process provides an excellent opportunity for the school counselor to manage change within their institutions and programs.

Benefits for School Counseling Programs

The school improvement/strategic planning process affords the professional school counselor an excellent opportunity to provide leadership through the use of facilitation skills to the entire school community. An integral part of the strategic planning is the identification of needs and desires of the school community.

The school counselor's involvement in the school improvement/ strategic planning process can impact the beliefs, mission, strategies, and outcomes of a building level improvement plan. The identification of school and school counseling program needs can be mutually beneficial. Conversely, the school counseling program must clearly enhance the school's mission, beliefs, and goals. A systematic planning process promotes accountability.

Conclusion

Strategic planning is a process for managing change in both school improvement and in comprehensive school counseling program development. In addition, operational planning is interfaced with strategic planning to define short term goals and objectives, program maintenance, and fiscal concerns. As a change agent the school counselor is well suited to serve as an effective facilitator of the strategic planning process.

References

Hayes, R. L., & Kormanski, C., et al. (Fall 1993). The school counselor and strategic planning: A skills development approach. New York State Association For Counseling and Development, pp. 71-76.

Lazotte, L. W. (1995). Building the total quality effective school: Idealized redesign. Iowa Effective Schools Conference, Melford, IA.

Olson, J. (Ed.). (1996). East High School Improvement Plan. Unpublished Document.

Senge, P. M., & Kleiner, A., et al. (1994). *The Fifth Discipline Fieldbook.* New York: Currency and Doubleday.

Jan Olson, NCC, NCSC, is a professional school counselor at East High in Sioux City, IA and former ASCA Secondary Vice President, 1992-1994. She is a consultant on school site improvement and strategic planning.

Jackie M. Allen, Ed.D, NCC, NCSC, MFCC is a school counselor and school psychologist and consultant with Allen Consulting Associates. She has been ASCA President, 1993-1994.

The Development of National Standards for School Counseling Programs

Carol A. Dahir

Overview

For years, school reform initiatives have been proposed and enacted in the name of achieving excellence in education. Relatively few areas of public education have escaped national attention, and yet, this has brought neither increased regard for, nor support of, guidance and counseling in the schools. Why have school counseling programs been largely overlooked? It may be the relatively small size of the counseling community or the poor public and professional understanding of the roles performed by school counselors (Burtnett, 1993).

The movement for acceptance of school counseling programs as a legitimate and recognized component of the educational system has been an uphill struggle by individuals, and national and state professional associations. Many years of ambiguity in the organization of guidance services has resulted in a lack of program focus, and guidance has been perceived as an ancillary service supplementing the academic goals of schooling (Gerler, 1992). Mathewson (1962) referred to guidance as a search for a system characterized by statements of objectives and goals. Ryan and Zeran (1972) suggested that guidance has suffered from a lack of systematic theory to guide the practical applications of services which significantly differ from the curriculum delivery of the academic disciplines. Drury (1984) placed the blame on counselors themselves for creating and poorly managing piecemeal programs which are dependent upon the interests of counselors. Halstead (1983) warned the profession that school counselors must take action to gain support for school counseling programs. This lack of a clear structure resulted in many new duties added to the counselor's existing responsibilities (Gysbers, 1990).

Since the late 1980s (Snyder & Daly, 1993), the counseling

profession has called for a revitalization and transformation in school counseling programs. Organizations that have an interest in the work of school counselors, such as the College Board and the National Association of College Admissions Counselors (NACAC), have advocated the reorganization of school counseling programs to meet the needs of all students.

Historically, the American School Counselor Association (ASCA) has established its positions and goals in statements that guide the practitioner in implementation. More specifically, the ASCA has published role definitions, a program philosophy, and monographs that speak to the role of guidance and counseling in the educational system. Yet, school counseling is still perceived to be an umbrella term encompassing a wide variety of services offered to students in kindergarten through high school (Gysbers & Henderson, 1988).

The educational movement enacted by Goals 2000 (1994) to design national standards and world-class benchmarks by the academic disciplines is intended to ensure that all graduates of our high schools and post-secondary institutions can compete in a global economy. Students and schools rise to the expectations that are established. The challenge also lies in providing all students with the appropriate conditions for learning to achieve at their maximum potential. Although national standards were legislated in nine different curriculum areas the role of school counseling programs as part of the educational process was not mentioned.

Standards Defined

The definition of standards has taken on a variety of meanings for the academic disciplines and for the associations involved in their development. Darling-Hammond (1992) suggested that standards for practice identify the overarching goals for an organization, thereby, establishing a direction for the practitioner. Eisner (1993) proposed several different meanings for standards: as targets or aims; as icons of student achievement; or as something common or typical. Wiggins (1991) defines a standard as an objective ideal, serving as a worthy and tangible goal for everyone, while Howe (1991) suggests standards must be perceived as reasonable levels of success that reflect our diverse society. Standards for what students should know and be able to do are currently transforming American education (Alexander, 1993).

Advocates of standards seek assurances that impoverished students or members of minority groups won't be denied an opportunity to learn. O'Neil (1993) questioned this unprecedented venture for American education by asking if it is really possible to help all students attain higher standards despite tremendous diversity and variability. Similarly, Brandt (1993) raised the concern that students will fail to meet unrealistic expectations.

Standards For School Counseling Programs

The School Counselor's Role In Educational Reform (ASCA, 1993) encouraged school counselors to become catalysts for educational change, and assume or accept, a leadership role in education reform. As specialists in child and adolescent development, school counselors coordinate the objectives, strategies, and activities of a comprehensive and developmental school counseling program to meet the personal, social, educational and career development needs of all students. School counselors advocate for students as students strive to meet the challenges and demands of the school system and prepare for transition to options after high school. School counselors call attention to situations in schools that are defeating or frustrating students and, thereby, hindering their success.

National standards for school counseling programs support the academic mission of the school by promoting and enhancing the learning process. School counseling programs contribute the essential personal, social, educational, and career development support for students to overcome obstacles to school achievement and to ensure access to appropriate services for students with varying individual needs (Wurtz, NEGP, 1995).

In accepting the challenge of the National Standards movement, the American School Counselor Association (July, 1994) passed a motion to undertake the process of developing voluntary national standards for school counseling programs. The ASCA's decision to develop national standards for school counseling programs offers an opportunity to the school counseling community to implement the goals deemed important by the profession and to promote its mission in education reform. Standards are not a new concept to the school counseling profession. In 1979, *Standards for Guidance and Counseling Programs* were approved by the Governing Board of the American School Counselor Association. These standards broadly defined the administrative structure, program resources and facilities, program review process and planning and evaluation guidelines for guidance and counseling programs. These program standards suggested consistency in practice while conforming to the individual school's philosophy of education. Standards also exist for ethical practices (ASCA, rev. 1994) and for obtaining a national certification (NBCC, 1986).

Rationale for National Standards for School Counseling

School counseling continues to have difficulty attaining precision in research due to the intangible nature of a counseling situation. Standards should be set so that counselors, administrators, and the general public understand what school counseling programs are today (Perry, 1991). Carlson (1991) concurred by suggesting that school counseling will continue to fight long and hard for survival until school counseling programs are effectively communicated to the public.

If the public is not cognizant of the role and function of counseling in the school setting, then the school counselor's role in supporting student learning clearly must be demonstrated. Gysbers and Henderson (1988) reminded us that school counseling programs do share similar characteristics with other educational programs, such as student outcomes, activities and processes to assist students in achieving these outcomes, and professionally recognized personnel, materials, and resources.

Can school counselors demonstrate that they are a significant positive force in the lives of children and in the school environment (Greer & Richardson, 1992)? Boyer (1988), in his description of the role of the school counselor stated:

> Today, in most high schools, counselors are not only expected to advise students about college, they are also asked to police for drugs, keep records of dropouts, reduce teenage pregnancy, check traffic in the halls, smooth out the tempers of irate parents, and give aid and comfort to battered and neglected children. School counselors are expected to do what our communities, our homes and our churches have not been able to accomplish, and if they cannot, we condemn them for failing to fulfill our high minded expectations (Exploring the Future, p.3).

Although interest in the broad objectives of guidance (and counseling) has grown in recent years, school counseling continues to be equated by many with individual counseling or it is considered as an ancillary administrative service. The school counseling community, almost 90,000 in the latest federal count, must clearly establish and articulate its purpose, goals, and its relationship to the educational system if it is to become an active participant in educational change.

National standards for school counseling programs:

- create a framework for a national model for school counseling programs;
- establish school counseling as an integral component of the academic mission of the educational system;
- encourage equitable access to school counseling services for all students provided by a certified school counselor;
- identify the key components of a comprehensive developmental school counseling model program;
- identify the knowledge and skills that all students should acquire as a result of the K - 12 School Counseling program; and
- ensure that school counseling programs are comprehensive in design and delivered in a systematic fashion to all students.

The Development Process for National Standards

School counseling is different from the academic disciplines. The development of national standards for school counseling programs required an examination of theory, research, and practice to ensure that all aspects of school counseling are considered. The process solicited a broad-based involvement from school counselors to communicate the purpose served by standards, as well as what standards school counseling programs should contain.

A pilot survey was distributed at the ASCA annual national delegate assembly in April, 1995, to assess the state and national leadership's attitudes and beliefs toward the development of national standards for school counseling programs. Responses received from the delegates in all fifty states overwhelmingly endorsed the concept for the development of national standards. Additionally, the leadership rated and suggested a variety of activities that could be included in school counseling program standards.

A statistically sound and sufficiently comprehensive data analysis was required to support the foundation for standards development. ACT, (American College Test) served as research consultant and coordinator for the collection of information and the company donated personnel and resources to ensure that the survey design, distribution, and data analysis followed universally accepted research practices.

A revised survey instrument was mailed in September, 1995,

to more than 2000 ASCA members who are currently employed as elementary, middle/junior high, high school counselors, and/or counselor supervisors. This sample provided essential information as to school counselor attitudes towards developing national standards for school counseling programs, the purpose that standards would serve, and what content areas should be included in the standards for school counseling programs.

The Results of the Membership Survey Revealed

School Counselors:
- want national standards;
- believe that national standards will resolve many of the problems that school counseling has confronted in establishing itself in the educational system;
- want national standards based more upon practice than theory; demonstrate that program priorities are based predominantly on work setting;
- maintain that national standards will organize the goals and body of knowledge that constitute a school counseling program;
- confirm that personal/social development is the most important component of a school counseling program for elementary, middle/junior high, and high school counselors;
- support an increased importance of educational and career development activities in national standards;
- and advocate system support activities that are directly connected to supporting or assisting students needs.

In summary, the development process for national standards included a national membership survey, a comprehensive analysis of the survey data, school counseling research, and literature, and a series of field reviews for ASCA members and other association leaders and members who have an interest in the work of school counselors. Publication and nationwide distribution is scheduled for June, 1997.

Conclusion

Research has demonstrated (Borders & Drury, 1992; Herr, 1984) that school counseling played an important role in shaping the design and implementation of programs and services that can best serve student needs. Literature has also evidenced that a unified perspective for school counseling programs could help to ensure that similar outcomes, opportunities, and experiences will be available to all students. The development of national standards significantly impacts the future of school counseling programs by clearly establishing and articulating the role and function school counseling serves within our nation's educational system.

National standards for school counseling programs will direct the vision and goals for school counseling into the twenty-first century. National standards will become the mechanism for the recognition of school counseling as a legitimate component of the educational system. National standards will connect the school counseling program to the educational mission of the school. Most importantly, national standards will establish similar goals, expectations, support systems and experiences for all students as a result of participation in school counseling programs. National standards can provide the framework for the delivery of high quality school counseling programs for all students. And, most importantly, the future of school counseling is defined by the practitioner, not redirected by others, as has been the pattern throughout the history of the profession.

References

Alexander, F. (1993, February). National standards: A new conventional wisdom. *Educational Leadership,* 9-10.

American School Counselor Association. (1979). *Standards for guidance and counseling programs.* Falls Church, Va.: American Personnel and Guidance Association.

American School Counselor Association. (1994). *The school counselor's role in educational reform.* Alexandria, Va.: ASCA Press.

Borders, L.D., & Drury, R.D. (1992). Comprehensive school counseling programs: A review for policy makers and practitioners. *Journal of Counseling and Development, 70* (4), 487-498.

Boyer, E. L. (1988). Exploring the future: Seeking new challenges. *Journal of College Admissions, 118,* 2 -8.

Brandt, R. (1993). Overview: Achieving higher standards. *Educational Leadership, 50,* (5),1.

Burtnett, F. (1993, April 28). Move counseling off the back burner of reform. *Education Week, 32,* 22.

Carlson, N. (1991). School counseling: Implementation and survival skills. *The School Counselor, 39,* (1), 30-34.

Darling-Hammond, L. (1992). *Standards of practice in learner-centered schools.* New York State Education Department. New York: NCREST.

Drury, S. S. (1984). Counselor survival in the 1980's. *School Counselor, 31,* 234-240.

Eisner, E.W. (1993, February). *Educational Leadership,* 22-24.

Gerler, E. (1992). What we know about school counseling: A reaction to Borders and Drury. *Journal of Counseling and Development, 70,* 499-500.

Greer, R., & Richardson, M. (1992). Restructuring the guidance delivery system: Implications for high school counselors. *School Counselor, 40,* 93-102.

Gysbers, N. (1990). *Comprehensive guidance programs that work.* Ann Arbor, MI.: ERIC/CAPS.

Gysbers, N., & Henderson, P. (1988). *Developing and managing your school guidance program.* Alexandria, Va: American Association for Counseling and Development.

Halstead, D. (1983). Counseling: Will it survive the 80's?, *School Guidance Worker, 39,* (2), 5-9.

Herr, E. L. (1984). The national reports on reform in schooling: Some missing ingredients. *Journal of Counseling and Development, 63,* 217-220.

Howe, H. (1991, November). America 2000: A bumpy ride on four trains. *Phi Delta Kappan,* 192-203.

Mathewson, R. H. (1962). *Guidance policy and practice.* New York: Harper & Bros.

Myrick, R. D. (1989). Developmental guidance and counseling: A practical approach. *Elementary Guidance and Counseling, 24,* (11), 14-20.

Myrick, R. D. (1993). *Developmental guidance and counseling: A practical approach.* Minneapolis: Educational Media Corporation.

National Education Goals Panel. (1994). *Building a nation of learners.* Washington, D.C..

O'Neil, J. (1993, February). Can national standards make a difference? *Educational Leadership.* 4-6.

Pennsylvania Department of Education. (1994). *Guiding and counseling youth...building for the future.* Harrisburg, Pa.

Perry, N. (1991). *School counseling outcomes and research.* Paper submitted to EDRS. Maine.

Ryan, T., & Zeran, F. (1972). *Organization and administration of guidance services.* Danville, Il.: Interstate.

Snyder, B., & Daly, P. (1993). Restructuring for guidance and counseling. *School Counselor, 41,* 37-43.

Wiggins, G. (1991). Standards, not standardization: Evoking quality student work. *Educational Leadership,* 18-25.

Wurtz, E. (1995). Phone conversation. National Education Goals Panel.

Carol Dahir has served the American School Counselor Association in a variety of leadership positions since 1990, most recently as Vice President for Post Secondary/Supervisor, Professional Development and Research Chair. Carol has undertaken the research design and methodology for the National Standards project and has collaborated with Chari Campbell, Ph.D., in the design and writing of the national standards document. Carol was instrumental in the development of the New York State Comprehensive Developmental School Counseling Model and as a supervisor of Pupil Personnel Services and Guidance and Counseling for the past ten years, has experienced the challenges of designing, implementing, articulating, and supervising school counseling programs.

School Counselor
Professionalism

Home, School, and Community Partnerships

Mary E. Gehrke

Overview

School counselors cannot stand alone or work in isolation if they are to be successful. In fact, partnerships are essential if counseling positions are to continue to be supported in schools. Students live in social units, whether it be in a family, the school, or the community at large. Since members of these social units all contribute to the development of the individual child, partnerships must be created in the homes of students, in the schools where school counselors practice their profession, and in the community at large, in order to work with the entire child. Partnerships provide an extended support system for the counseling and guidance program and enhance student success.

Home Partnerships

Partnerships with the parents and guardians of the students are vital. The term "parent" as used here, includes biological parents, adoptive parents, and legally appointed guardians. Almost all of the students that school counselors serve are minors, and as children, they are under the control and authority of their parents. School counselors cannot have a significant impact on the lives of students unless there is support and positive intervention at home.

Unfortunately, schools cannot ensure that the adults in children's lives are fulfilling their child rearing responsibilities. Although schools cannot take over the parenting process they can provide parent effectiveness training and schools must partner with parents for the benefit of children.

There are some basic principles that school counselors who create effective home partnerships follow:

- School counselors acknowledge that parents have a right to teach their children values and beliefs that may be

different from those of the mainstream.
- Parents are informed of services that school counselors can and cannot offer.
- Parents are included to the maximum degree possible in the intervention process when children are in trouble.
- Some type of school-sponsored curriculum is offered to help parents learn effective parenting skills.
- Parents are regularly consulted regarding the school counseling program and their responses are seriously considered as the program is periodically adjusted.
- It is recognized that in today's homes, often there are adults other than parents, such as grandparents or step-parents, who are involved in the parenting of children.

School Partnerships

Partnerships are essential within the schools if counseling programs are to enjoy success and support. Gone are the days when school counselors could isolate themselves under a stack of paperwork or spend hours of time with individual counseling appointments. The negative image of a school counselor isolated from the rest of the school community alone in an office with a coffee cup cannot be perpetuated. The school counselor must be aware of the daily stresses felt by teachers and administrators.

Effective school counselors are seen by teachers and administrators as being a vital partner in the educational team. School counselors who have created successful partnerships with teachers and administrators are recognized for the unique knowledge they possess and are valued for their willingness to be a part of the school team. School counselors need to assert themselves, however, to ensure that their special contributions are acknowledged as significantly different from the contributions of teachers and administrators.

School partnerships with teachers and administrators seem natural to successful counselors. To determine whether the school counselor is successful in creating such partnerships, the following questions may be asked:
- Does the school counselor value the essential educational tasks of teachers and administrators?
- Does the school counselor give a written list of services that can and cannot be provided to teachers and administrators?
- Does the school counselor make every effort to inform

teachers and administrators of the problems of students so that teachers and administrators can do their jobs effectively?

- Does the school counselor provide in-service training for teachers and administrators to help them deal effectively with counseling-related matters?
- Does the school counselor ask teachers and administrators to evaluate the effectiveness of the school counseling program on a regular basis?

An incredibly gifted and conscientious school counselor who has failed to establish positive partnerships with teacher and administrator colleagues cannot be effective. School counselors do not function in isolation. They depend upon the support and collaboration of teachers and administrators.

Community Partnerships

The community partnership developed by successful school counselors is as important as the relationships counselors establish in homes and within schools. The children who are served in school counseling programs come from the community, live in the community while they attend school, and will one day contribute to the community as educated citizens.

The most important community partnerships established by school counselors are those developed with professionals in the community who provide counseling services that are beyond the capacity of the school. School counselors need to know who in the community can diagnose and provide physical and mental health services. In addition, school counselors need to know what other resources in the community can provide counseling-related services including, but not limited to, personal support, subject matter tutoring, college placement assistance, school-to-work transition, or other programs for youth. Along with community partnerships for counselors comes the challenge of appropriate ethical and professional referrals.

An effective school counselor-community partnership should include the following:

- A planned outreach program in which school counselors establish relationships with professionals in the community who can provide counseling and counseling-related services.
- The development and continual updating of a community

resource directory.

- A system within the counseling program for obtaining permission from students and their parents to share information between school counselors and community professionals.
- An orientation and follow-up program for students and parents who are referred to an outside resource for services.

In addition to the routine practice of establishing partnerships with community professionals and agencies that provide counseling-related services, school counselors need to make efforts to create other community partnerships. It is vital that community members know the important nature of school counseling programs, understand the goals of such programs, and develop a commitment to support school counseling efforts. Essential community partnerships include those with local elected officials; with business leaders who have financial resources with which they could support school counseling programs; with law enforcement officers, child protective services professionals, and other governmental agency personnel; and with media representatives who have the means to inform the public and can help shape public opinion regarding counseling programs.

Conclusion

Partnerships are an important part of a school guidance and counseling program. Home partnerships assist parents in the important process of parenting. School partnerships form a collaborative relationship with school staff to work for student success. Community partnerships provide an organized and coordinated outreach program to access and use a variety of community resources. Effective partnerships with home, school, and community are essential for the success of contemporary school counselors.

References

Allen, J. (1994). *School counselors collaborating for student success.* ERIC Clearinghouse on Counseling and Student Services. Greensboro, NC: (EDO-CG-94-27)

American School Counselor Association. (1994). *National school counseling week kit: A partnership in caring.* Alexandria, VA: Author.

American School Counselor Association. (1995). *School counseling today: School, home, community.* Alexandria, VA: Author.

Mary E. Gehrke, NCC, NCSC, is a school counselor in the Racine Unified School District in Racine, Wisconsin and served as the 1994-1995 American School Counselor Association President.

22

Writing and Publishing for the School Counselor

Pat Nellor Wickwire

Overview

Writing for publication is an opportunity—and a responsibility—of the school counselor. Other professional counselors want to know what works in counseling.

The public wants to know what counselors do. Letting others know about successes and accomplishments in counseling programs and services is imperative for the counseling profession.

People write for many different reasons: to inform, report, and record; to clarify, describe, and explain; to express, persuade, and captivate; to create, lead, and challenge; to solve, resolve, and neutralize; to connect, commit, and advocate; and to expose, question, and equivocate.

People write for many different publications: journals, magazines, newspapers, newsletters, radio, television, and theatre. They write brochures, flyers, and bulletins; books and scripts; reports and monographs; pamphlets, digests, and booklets; handbooks and manuals; audiotapes and videotapes; compact disks; and software. They write letters to editors, columns, editorials, book reviews, straight news, news features, features, interview articles, narratives, anecdotes, essays, and graphic-pictorial representations. They write expository, conceptual, and research manuscripts; literature reviews; historical snapshots; project proposals; and media kits. They write fiction and nonfiction. And, in the 1990s, people write electronic communications.

All of these reasons and vehicles for communication are available to the school counselor who seeks to advance the profession and to increase public awareness.

The Topic

The very first step in writing—and, some say, the most important step—is to select the topic. The aspiring writer asks:

"What is my passion? What ideas do I want or need others to know about? What have I done that others want or need to know about? Is there something I must do that writing will support?"

The next step is obvious: to write—and write, and write, and write. This is the time when the writer expresses passion, targets the purposes for writing, considers all to be said about the topic, and considers possible audiences. This is not the time to edit; that comes later.

The Readers

After choosing and drafting the core of the message, the writer identifies the target readers—the professionals or the public with interest and need for the information and the ideas. In school counseling, numerous potential readers are present: counselor educators, community college and university counselors, mental health counselors, marriage and family counselors, career and employment counselors, substance abuse counselors, group counseling specialists, assessment and evaluation specialists, multicultural counseling specialists, school counselors, social workers, psychologists, teachers, administrators, career and vocational specialists, reading specialists, physical fitness and sports specialists, school board members, students, parents, community leaders, professional associations, industry and labor representatives, corporate and business executives, community agencies, educational institutions, citizens, and the general public.

The Publications

Next the writer identifies the vehicles to carry the message. Numerous publications are available to receive manuscripts about school counseling. Most national counseling and human services associations offer newsletters and professional journals, and some publish books and monographs. Many local, regional, and community newspapers are open for receipt of announcements, op-ed pieces, and news stories. *The Writer's Handbook* (Burack, 1995) alone includes 3,000 markets for nonfiction and fiction manuscripts. Self-publishing is also an option (Poynter, 1993).

Most publications have stylebooks or stylesheets that are available for purchase or are complimentary upon request; style and form are important for consistency and readability of publications (Strunk & White, 1979; Sutcliffe, 1994). Styles are different for different types of publications, for example, for newspaper journalism (United Press International, 1993). Most journals in the counseling and human development profession use APA style (American Psychological Association, 1994), and some use Chicago style (University of Chicago Press, 1993). Additionally, some publishing companies require letters of inquiry and, as in the case of books, written proposals with specific content and organization (Henson, 1995). The well-advised writer obtains information about style and other guidelines and requirements before beginning to edit for manuscript submission. The savvy writer increases chances of manuscript acceptance by studying copies of publications for actual applications of requirements.

The Published Author

The writer who wants to become a published author prepares a reader-friendly, publication-friendly, profession-friendly, publishable manuscript. In addition to following the conventions for acceptable writing and the necessary guidelines for publication, the writer observes legal requirements, ethics, and standards of conduct, such as submitting a single manuscript to one publication at a time, using nonbiased language, maintaining confidentiality, giving credit to other authors, and informing of the limitations of research. The writer responds with exactness and promptness to the recommendations and requests of editors and publishers. Both attitude and craft are essential in the intensely personal yet tool-oriented experience of writing and publishing (Zinsser, 1994).

The writer who wants to become a published author prepares a streamlined final draft of a manuscript, with attention to tone, viewpoint, timing, timeliness, length, vocabulary, focus, form, and other areas. The writer knows that the manuscript will be evaluated on content, organization, presentation, and other factors, including impact, appropriateness, contribution to knowledge, purpose, meaningfulness, orderliness, readability, accuracy, and writing style—and that some of these will be unique to a publication. For example, professional journals are usually refereed, that is, panels of peers read and rate blind manuscripts anonymously against specified criteria; recommendations of these panels can be invaluable for revision and creation of a successful publication. And, for example, newspapers usually require timeliness; short sentences; the use of "down" style, with fewer capital letters; inclusion of who, what, when, where, why, how, and how much; the use of inverted pyramid style, with information in declining order of importance; appeal to the general public; pages that are not stapled; and the use of -30- to mark the end of copy. The writer who submits clean and clear copy, and who satisfies unique publication needs and expectations, increases the chance of becoming a published author.

The School Counselor as a Published Author

The school counselor who is a published author contributes to the advancement and enhancement of the profession and to the increase in public awareness and appreciation of the profession. The school counselor can write about successful programs and services, accomplishments of students and staff, uses and needs for funding, community relationships, parent support, student growth, staff collaboration, professional advances, and special events. The school counselor can inform, clarify, lead, and advocate. The school counselor can present solutions, create connections, influence action, initiate change, express opinions, establish records, identify resources, and carry out a host of other actions through writing and publishing. The school counselor with a forward plan, a future book, and written connections with the public and with the profession can contribute immeasurably to human development.

Conclusion

Many opportunities are available to inform others and to promote the causes of school counseling through the written word. The school counselor who takes the challenge, the opportunity, and the responsibility of writing and publishing, accrues and enjoys many rewards. The school counselor who is a published author makes an impact on the foundations of knowledge in the profession and an impact on the public understanding of the accomplishments of the profession.

References

American Psychological Association. (1994). *Publication manual of the American Psychological Association* (4th ed.). Washington, DC: Author.

Burack, S. K. (Ed.). (1995). *The writer's handbook.* Boston: The Writer.

Henson, K. T. (1995). *The art of writing for publication.* Boston: Allyn and Bacon.

Poynter, D. (1993). *The self-publishing manual: How to write, print and sell your own book* (7th ed.). Santa Barbara, CA: Para Publishing.

Strunk, W., Jr., & White, E. B. (1979). *The elements of style* (3rd ed.). New York: Macmillan.

Sutcliffe, A. J. (Ed.). (1994). *The New York Public Library writer's guide to style and usage.* New York: Harper Collins.

United Press International. (1993). *UPI stylebook: The authoritative handbook for writers, editors & news directors* (3rd ed.). Lincolnwood, IL: National Textbook Company.

University of Chicago Press. (1993). *The Chicago manual of style: The essential guide for writers, editors, and publishers* (14th ed.). Chicago: Author.

Zinsser, W. K. (1994). *On writing well: An informal guide to writing nonfiction* (5th ed.). New York: Harper Collins.

Pat Nellor Wickwire, Ph.D., NCC, LEP, MFCC, is President, The Nellor Wickwire Group, Hermosa Beach, California; Editor, California Association for Counseling and Development Journal; and Media Chairperson, National Career Development Association.

23

Total Quality Leadership and School Counseling

Rebecca M. Dedmond

Overview

Today's educational external customers (parents, community members, employees) are demanding that educators equip students (internal students) with quality tools to deal with the changing world. A quality-improvement process needs to be in place now in order to identify improvement in the educational system. New methods and systems must be in place in order to provide the highest quality education. While the commitment to quality improvement must begin with those in leadership positions who have the power to make it happen, school counselors, who are specialists in changing human behavior, become natural leaders in the initiative.

Continuous improvement should be the focus of all school programs. The ultimate goal is for students who can think, learn, and perform in and across traditional and emerging subjects and program areas.

The Definition of Quality

Quality means conformance to all customer (students, parents, community) requirements. Quality organizations contend that the organization is successful only if its customers are satisfied. In education this translates to the following goal: the school is successful if all students have learned to their maximum potential. Learning means they can demonstrate what they have mastered. (Burgess & Dedmond, 1994)

Quality means continuous improvement, not a one-time effort. Continuous improvement is supported by an integrated system of tools, techniques, and training. It is built into the management of the organization and it defines the organization's culture.

Quality Principles

Quality is a set of principles that focus on the needs of an organization's customers and that find ways to continuously improve the work processes that make up the system. In quality organizations, self-managed teams measure and monitor their own work processes, with the goal of customer satisfaction driving their efforts (Burgess, 1992).

When adapted and implemented, quality principles:
- improve work processes
- enhance productivity of all involved
- result in productive, involved workers
- create customers who are better satisfied.

Quality Tools

Quality tools include data gathering and utilization, which are critical to all problem-solving efforts. Charts and diagrams are two of the tools used to develop, define, and identify problems. Displaying data ensures that the focus is shifted from results and is placed on improvement of the systems that create the results. The system of education involves many interrelated subsystems, all focused on a common goal.

Quality Leadership

Total Quality Leadership is defined as follows:

Total: All employees are committed to customer satisfaction and continuous improvement of processes.
Quality: Satisfaction of all customers.
Leadership: Leadership that listens to and empowers employees in a workplace environment of trust; aligns with customers and focuses on their needs; measures critical work processes in order to continuously improve products and services.

Quality improvement requires a change in attitude, or a new philosophy of management. Development of a management philosophy that values continuous learning is essential. Management must build trust in order to create the necessary teamwork in the organization. Trust can be won throughout the school only by a fundamental shift in working relationships.

The key to any school becoming a quality organization is its ability to cause all employees to communicate and work together (in self-managed teams). Creation of new partnerships among employees enables and empowers them to make work-related decisions to improve the quality of their services to customers. Quality is a way of thinking and working to achieve continuous improvement through the involvement of all employees in the school system and through a focus on the needs and satisfaction of customers—students, parents, and community.

The professional school counselor brings unique knowledge and skills to the change process that make them leaders in every facet of quality. The counselor can ensure the successful participation of all employees in the organization by employing quality guidance principles, including communication, collaboration, coordination, facilitation, cooperation, problem solving, information and resources gathering, team building, assessment and evaluation, and enhancement of people skills. The strategy provides team members with a means to help decision makers consider, plan for, and implement policy and process changes that affect education and student achievement in the local school division.

Counselors may become involved in the Quality movement by taking leadership responsibilities for the following tasks:

- provide input into curriculum development, based on analysis and synthesis of the needs of students, parents, and community;
- provide staff development, based on identified needs of educators as related to needs of students, parents, and community;
- establish an advisory committee, in order to gain input on educational processes from external customers;
- implement a quality communication system, by building teams of teachers, teams of administrators, teams of students, teams of community members, and teams of a combination of each;
- set goals and measure, based on charted or graphed data gathered about goals and progress;
- identify and eliminate problems as stated by both internal and external customers;
- research and develop new initiatives that have worked for schools and programs with similar demographics
- create a structure for employee involvement by determining areas of interest and expertise of each, and teams in which they are willing to lead or

participate;

- recognize, reward, and celebrate successes, improvements, changes that lead to improvement of the system, and desired outcomes;
- link to the community by involving citizens on advisory councils, in planning for change, in determining best practices, and in other areas in which they have established good management and leadership practices;
- strive for continuous improvement of all practices and processes in the school and the community of the school.

Leadership Attributes—What Works?

Counselors provide a service as they utilize their expertise and as they lead school improvement teams. Counselors can:

Create a mutually agreed upon vision. The vision must address the goals that the schools, parents, and community have for students. The vision must be inherent in the school philosophy and should reflect the assessed needs of students and the entire community.

Build a collaborative effort. It is critical that counselors have help as they address the formidable tasks of today. They use their networking skills to convene key persons into groups that support the vision and mission of the school. School administrators, classroom teachers, members of the community, business and government must all contribute to the leadership, expertise, facilities, funds, materials, and information.

Select the right tools and relevant methods to gather new information. Counselors know how to gather data on students' needs, community needs, programs that work, test and progress data, and other information, and then present it graphically in useful charts and graphs. Data will likely be utilized to redesign and modify processes, practices, and programs that best serve the needs of each student and the entire school.

Successful improvement programs are led by counselors who are willing to take a risk and get things done.

Counselors are needed who are energetic, flexible, and highly motivated to help students.

- They create comprehensive programs that bridge the relationship among school subjects, programs that will be used by students both today and in their futures.
- They develop new services, programs, relationships, and rules.
- They encourage team building and can contribute, as well as solicit, suggestions, tools, and information from others in order to make the process work better.
- They have the ability to forge connections between educational and community interests
- They understand the need to access and utilize the vast amount of information available.

It is critical that counselors take a proactive role in the quality movement in order to improve counseling programs, raise student expectations and goals, and enhance the entire school curriculum and program. For the internal customers (the students) it is the counselor's responsibility to strive to raise standards and to assist them, along with their parents, to become motivated to achieve. For other internal customers (other educators) and external customers (parents and the community), restructuring systems to meet society's needs is the ultimate goal. Counselors can play a leadership role in the most critical process of all—the change process.

References

American Association of School Administrators. (1991). *An introduction to total quality for schools: A collection of articles on the concepts of total quality management and W. Edwards Deming.* Arlington, VA: AASA.

American Association of School Administrators. (1992). *Creating quality schools.* Arlington, VA: AASA.

Burgess, D. (1992). Who are the customers of school counselors? *The ASCA Counselor, 29*(5), 8.

Burgess, D., & Dedmond, R. (1994). *Quality leadership and the professional school counselor.* (Alexandria, VA:) American School Counselor Association.

Office of Educational Research and Improvement, United
States Department of Education. *Toward Quality in
Education: The Leader's Odyssey.*

Rebecca M. Dedmond, Ph.D., LPC.

Credentialing and Certification for School Counselors

John W. Bloom & Susan Eubanks

Overview

School counselors as well as graduate students and counselor educators in school counseling programs usually are familiar with why and how state departments of education certify school counselors, but are often puzzled about the rest of the school counselor credentialing picture. School counselors want to know if they should obtain a Licensed, Certified, or Registered Professional Counselor credential (LPC, CPC, or RPC) from their state and if they should obtain the National Certified Counselor or National Certified School Counselor credential (NCC or NCSC) from the National Board for Certified Counselors, Inc. (NBCC).

This section will examine briefly the current status of state department of education credentialing processes and then address concerns related to the LPC, NCC and NCSC credentials. Also, for more information than can be presented here, the reader's attention is directed to a recent, and still current, comprehensive article, *The School Counselor and Credentialing* (Clawson, 1993) as well as to other references used in the preparation of this chapter.

State Department of Education Certification

In every state, professional school counselors are required by law and/or regulation to obtain a state-issued credential in order to be employed in public schools, whether the credential be called "certification," "licensure," or "endorsement" (Farrell, 1996). However, state department of education credentialing standards are *minimal* standards. This becomes apparent when comparing state department standards with CACREP (Council for the Accreditation of Counseling and Related Educational Programs) standards.

CACREP says that school counseling programs must include a minimum of 48 semester hours of graduate work in counseling

(CACREP, 1994). However, only 40 states even require the completion of a master's degree in counseling and guidance or a related field and even fewer states (22) require the completion of a specific minimum number of credit hours of graduate study in guidance and counseling before being credentialed. The number of required hours ranges from 18 to 44 semester hours with fifteen states requiring completion of 30 or more semester hours (Farrell, 1996).

A recent trend in some states like Arizona, toward the formation of publicly funded charter schools which operate with a minimum of government interference, creates additional concern (Arizona Daily Sun, July 7, 1996). The more than 100 Arizona charter schools rarely have school counselors and, in the few instances they do, those counselors may or may not be state department certified or endorsed.

Finally, state department certification standards are often determined with minimal input from school counselors, school counselor professional membership organizations, or professional counselor credentialing or accreditation bodies. State departments are much more responsive to the wants and needs of school administrators who must strike a reasonable balance between the need for excellence in certification standards and the need to be able to attract qualified individuals to work in less desirable locations. Stringent certification standards would often mean significantly reducing the applicant pool in such areas.

Thus having a state department of education school counselor certificate, endorsement, or license ensures one's ability to be employed as school counselor, but it is rarely an indication of a professional level of competence. Could it become the latter? Yes, if counselors work closely with certification policy makers and explain to them the ethical and legal ramifications, along with the educational benefits, of hiring more highly qualified practitioners. No, if counselors are reluctant to become involved in the politics of education.

State Professional Counselor Credentialing

The best way to "show your publics" that you are indeed a professional with more than minimal competencies is to seek appropriate state and national credentialing. This is a major part of being a "professional" in the true sense of the word (Clawson, 1993).

Historically, school counselors have not only supported their private sector colleagues' legislative efforts to obtain licensure, but have also obtained LPC and NCC credentials in somewhat surprising numbers (Geisler, 1994; Clawson, 1993). Speculation is that school counselors realize that, in states where they are eligible for the LPC, now is the best time to obtain the credential because requirements rarely become less stringent.

School counselors may also realize that having the LPC credential may give more flexibility in the marketplace. School counselors may want to practice privately during extended vacation periods or in the evening, may want to be prepared for possible school reductions in force, and may want to plan job shifts for their retirement years. And who knows when insurance companies may recognize school counselors who are also LPCs as eligible for third party payments.

National Counselor Certification

NBCC is the largest national master's level counselor credentialing body. Since the greatest number of NCCs are school counselors, clearly the NCC credential fills a need for school counselors not met by a state department of education or an LPC credential. Perhaps school counselors, who are often in that no man's land between teachers and administrators, have a need for the recognition that a national credential brings. They may also take pride in knowing that they are supporting the efforts of NBCC to further the cause of all counselors in legislative, credentialing, and political venues. The fact that one exam, the National Counseling Examination for Licensure and Certification (NCE), meets the requirements for both the NCC and (in 36 states) the LPC, makes it convenient and prudent for the school counselor to obtain both credentials without having to take two exams.

National School Counseling Specialty Certification

Currently more than 700 NCCs also hold the National Certified School Counselor (NCSC) specialty certification. The school counseling specialty area originally emerged, and continues to evolve, as a result of social, educational, political, and economic trends (Paisley & Borders, 1995). NBCC's philosophy is that all professional counselors have common coursework and supervised experiences as reflected in CACREP preparation standards and ultimately in NCC certification requirements. These common bonds help unify the school counselor with the gerontological counselor, the addictions counselor, the clinical mental health counselor, and the career counselor, as well as with the professional counselor in general practice.

The NCSC specialty credential is a result of joint efforts of the American Counseling Association, the American School Counselor Association, and the National Board for Certified Counselors. The NCSC, the first national school counselor specialty credential established in 1992, attests to the educational background, skills, and competencies of the specialist in schoolcounseling (NBCC, 1996). Requirements for the NCSC include supervised professional counseling experience in a school setting, specialized school counseling coursework, a written self-assessment, and two professional assessments. An additional examination is not required for this specialty certification at this time.

The purposes of the national school counselor certification are to:

- Promote the school counselor's professional identity, visibility, and accountability on a national level.
- Identify to the counseling profession and to the public those counselors who have met national professional school counseling standards.
- Advance cooperation among school systems, professional organizations, and other credentialing professional development organizations.
- Encourage the professional growth of school counselors.

It is part of NBCC's long-range plan to propose to state boards of education that the NCSC be adopted in each state as an "alternative" method to gain state school counselor endorsement (Clawson, 1993). New Mexico has such a process in place and other states are currently considering adopting such an option.

These purposes also apply to counselor educators in school counseling graduate degree programs, however, recent research indicates that only 19% of faculty members are NCCs (NBCC, 1996). Surely what is good for the...well, you know the rest!

Conclusion

Test anxiety, cost, and rising credentialing requirements are frequently cited as barriers to certification and licensure. Test anxiety is an issue in almost any credentialing process. Many CACREP approved programs and some non-CACREP approved programs offer the NCE to students in the last semester of graduate study. Graduate students should take advantage of this opportunity because test anxiety increases over time and one's knowledge base decreases the longer one is removed from one's graduate studies.

Balancing the cost of credentialing processes with the cost of tuition, textbooks, and living expenses is problematic for many graduate students. Similarly, balancing credentialing costs with the cost of teacher union dues, continuing education, graduate study, and family expenses is difficult for many practicing school counselors. The cost of being fully professional often does put a strain on one's budget, but there is also a significant personal and professional cost to the profession of not being credentialed.

Finally, certification and licensure requirements almost always become more stringent over time. This is another reason to start the credentialing process sooner rather than later. As standards rise, professional counselors in the field may run the risk of having more supervised hours, more continuing education hours, and more graduate credit hours imposed upon them.

References

Bloom, J. (1996). *Credentialing counselors for the 21st century*. Greensboro, NC.

Clawson, T. (1993). The school counselor and credentialing. In J. Wittmer (Ed.), *Managing your school counseling program* (pp. 262-267). Minneapolis, MN: Educational Media Corporation.

Council for Accreditation of Counseling and Related Educational Programs. (1994). *CACREP accreditation standards and procedures manual*. Alexandria, VA: Author.

Farrell, P. (1996). *A guide to state laws and regulations of professional school counselors*. Alexandria, VA: The American Counseling Association.

Geisler, J. (1994). The impact of the passage of the Michigan counselor licensure law: One state's experience. *Journal of Mental Health Counseling, 12,* 188-198.

National Board for Certified Counselors, Inc. (1996). *Become certified in your counseling specialty by NBCC*. Greensboro, NC: Author.

Paisley, P. & Borders, D. (1995). School counseling: An evolving specialty. *Journal of Counseling & Development, 74,* 150-153.

Percy, R. (1996). *Teaching experience for school counselors revisited: An alternative certification model* . (ERIC Document Reproduction Service No. EDO-GC-96-39a and 39b.)

New world for charter schools. Editorial, Arizona Daily Sun, Flagstaff, AZ July 7, 1996

John W. Bloom, Ph.D., NCC, is Professor, Counselor Education, Butler University, Indianapolis, Indiana and Immediate Past Chair of the Board of Directors of the National Board for Certified Counselors.

Susan Eubanks, MA, is Director of Professional Relations, National Board for Certified Counselors, Inc., Greensboro, North Carolina.

25

Counseling and Guidance Advisory Councils

Fran Carney

Overview

A portion of the Arizona Comprehensive Competency Based Guidance Model (CCBG) is the Advisory Council. The selection and role of this committee is a necessary component of all successful counseling and guidance programs. The role of the Guidance Advisory Council is to "assist in developing a school competency-based guidance model and to assist in continuous evaluation, revision and improvement of the program" (ADE, 1991, p. 91).

History

As far back as 1976, Guidance Advisory Councils were identified as an effective strategy in identifying school district guidance goals and in recommending priorities for guidance and counseling. Even then, funding for support programs was becoming more and more precarious, and the mode of dealing with one student at a time on a continuous basis, began to be viewed as too costly. To survive, a shift in thinking and practice occurred, which also directed students and community members to share in the responsibility of identifying student guidance goals and outcomes. At that time, the most efficient means to accomplish such a task was to form and implement a Guidance Advisory Council. In Mesa, Arizona, as part of an ESEA Title III Project, a Competency-Based Staff Development Training Package was developed by district staff under the direction of Byron McKinnon, Director of Guidance, which addressed the establishment of Guidance Advisory Councils. Although incomplete, a draft document describing this process was begun by Sharon Crosson (Johnson), C. J. (Curly) Johnson and Duane Richins.

As the importance of CCBG programs grew and was recognized by the Arizona Department of Education, the Advisory Council concept continued as one of the twelve program elements of

Arizona's CCBG model. Marana Public School District, Marana Arizona, was used as the state model for developing and implementing a Guidance and Counseling Advisory Council. Consisting of volunteers from the community at large, the Council successfully promoted constructive change in the Marana Guidance and Counseling program (see the Holaway CCBG Digest).

During the early 1990s several additional school districts across the state of Arizona developed and implemented Guidance Advisory Councils. In Mesa, Arizona, however, the Guidance Advisory Councils of the mid-1970s had been absorbed by site-advisory councils. Then during the 1992-93 school year, Mesa Public Schools conducted a counseling and guidance strategic curriculum review, which recreated the Guidance Advisory model. A Guidance Review Committee was formed by volunteers representing Mesa Public Schools, business and industry, parents, students, Mesa Education Association, Arizona School Counselors Association, American Counseling Association, and Mesa Public Schools administrators. The committee reviewed the historical perspective of the Guidance Program in Mesa Public Schools, the issues and trends for the 21st Century, and rethought, revised and approved Mesa's Competency-Based Guidance Curriculum. The Mesa Public Schools Student Outcome-Based Counseling and Guidance Program was presented to the Governing Board, March 9, 1993.

Implementation

The first step in developing a Guidance Advisory Council is to identify the need for such a group. The formation of a competency-based guidance program requires this type of support to effectively develop and implement the philosophy, goals, competencies, management system, and school plans for the CCBG model. The guidance department and counselors who committed to the CCBG concept should first agree on the development of the Guidance Advisory Council and one counselor should be identified who will specifically be in charge of facilitating the Council. Administrative approval and support of the Guidance Advisory Council is an initial part of the process. A meeting should be scheduled with necessary administrators at the building and/or district level. A presentation of the purpose, the membership composition of the council, schedule of meetings, governing board presentation, and proposed agendas should be addressed.

After administrative approval is obtained, further discussion of the qualifications of advisory members should be discussed.

Guidance personnel, administrators, former students, parents, local employers, teachers, representatives for handicapped individuals, racial minorities, ethnic minorities, and various age levels should be included, if possible. The size of the council should be determined by the size of the community and the purpose of the council. It should be large enough to truly represent the school and community population,yet small enough to be managed effectively. Motivated individuals should be sought who are willing to devote time and effort required to complete the task. Members should be familiar with both the needs of the school and of the community at large.

The counselor in charge of the Guidance Advisory Committee should personally telephone the prospective members to request their participation. The telephone contact should be followed by a letter of appointment. A reminder call to members before each meeting is helpful as attendance at meetings is critical to the success of the council. Meeting dates should be projected annually, if possible. If the council meets on an on-going basis, a yearly planning work session is suggested to set dates and times of meetings as well as yearly goals. Several days before the Guidance Advisory Council meeting arrangements should be confirmed and an agenda prepared. The meeting room should be large enough to accommodate all in attendance and audio/visual equipment should be in working order.

Some additional adjustments may be in order to promote attendance and to ensure smoothly run meetings. The time of day for meetings will need to be addressed as well as the possibility of child care. Refreshments are always a welcome addition!

The Guidance Advisory Council Meeting

An agenda should be prepared for each meeting, including a time limit for speakers and presentations. Those individuals who are listed on the agenda should be informed in advance as to when they are scheduled to speak and their time allotment. Caution should be taken to keep the meeting times to a reasonable length. When the time limit is up, items under discussion should be tabled until the next meeting, or an additional meeting arranged to discuss a particular topic. It is also advantageous to involve the Guidance Advisory Council with other parent advisory groups. Advocacy should be promoted and collegial relationships developed throughout the school and community.

The first meeting of the council should provide for a get-acquainted activity. A presentation of the existing Guidance and Counseling program should be included. Guidance and Counseling goals for the current school year should be discussed, including a timeline for the Guidance Advisory Council. Brainstorming is recommended to identify concerns and important considerations for the Council. A team approach and consensus should be stressed. Care should be taken not to make the program so wide in scope that goals are unrealistic. An Action Plan for the Guidance Advisory Council should reflect the philosophy and goals (the cornerstones) of the Counseling and Guidance department (Trotter, 1992).

Conclusion

Looking toward the future, Guidance and Counseling programs across the country will be competing for funding and support from school boards and other sources of revenue within their community (Johnson & Whitfield, 1991). Guidance Advisory Councils that can serve as vehicles to monitor guidance programs and can recommend priorities to school and community leaders will increase the visibility of counseling and guidance programs, as well as provide advocacy for the importance of counseling and guidance activities and opportunities for students.

References

ADE [Arizona Department of Education] (1991). *Arizona comprehensive competency-based guidance program handbook*. Phoenix, AZ: Author

Johnson, S. K., & Whitfield, E. A. (1991). *Evaluating guidance programs: A practitioner's guide*. A joint project of American College Testing and The National Consortium of State Career Supervisors.

Trotter, T. V. (1992). *Walking the talk: Developing a local comprehensive school counseling program*. Alexandria, VA: American School Counselor Association.

Fran Carney, M.A., CPC, is the Director of Guidance and Counseling, Mesa Public Schools, Mesa, AZ.

26

Developing Assessment Standards for School Counselors

William D. Schafer & Barbara Webster

Overview

Assessments are used by virtually every education professional in virtually every school. Teachers use them to help guide instruction and to evaluate learning outcomes. Administrators (e.g., principals) use them to make decisions about individual students and policy. And counselors use them in three fundamental areas: pupil assessment, program evaluation, and research (Schafer, 1995).

Among these school professionals, counselors appear to be the most knowledgeable in the area of assessments (Impara, 1995). With 97.9% of institutions requiring assessment coursework in their professional preparation programs, school counselors are most likely to have studied assessment (Schafer & Lissitz, 1987). But little literature is available to describe the assessment understandings school counselors should have compared with the degree of specificity available for teachers (AFT, NCME, & NEA, 1990) and administrators (AASA, NAESP, NASSP, & NCME, 1994).

In designing or evaluating school counselor preparation programs, a description of specific content would enable a direct comparison of intended outcomes with expectations. Providers of continuing education would be able to focus on important assessment skills. Counseling students would have a description of the assessment outcomes they are expected to achieve, allowing them to engage in informed self-assessment as they learn. Those who certify and employ school counselors would have a clear description of needed competencies. Counselors, themselves, would be able to evaluate their own needs for continuing education and select opportunities most likely to allow meaningful professional growth.

The purpose of this chapter is to use two perspectives to review expectations for school counselors in assessment: the Council for the Accreditation of Counseling and Related Educational Programs

(CACREP, 1994) program standards and state certification standards. Suggestions for school counseling skills that could lead to improved assessment uses are then discussed.

Of course, current counselor education programs were not designed with these principles in mind. Neither have current school counseling practitioners typically studied all these areas of content. We present our suggestions with the understanding that they are best viewed now as aspirations, but we hope that they can in the future become expectations.

CACREP Standards

CACREP, a corporate affiliate of the American Counseling Association, accredits programs at higher education institutions. As of July, 1996, there were approved programs at 109 institutions in the United States (CACREP, personal communication, July 18, 1996).

Two of CACREP's eight core-curriculum areas, required for all counseling students in an approved program, apply to assessment. One core-curriculum area is appraisal. To satisfy the standards, a program must include the study of assessment and evaluation for both individuals and groups. Specifically mentioned are reliability; validity; specific techniques; computer assessment; types of scores; univariate and bivariate statistics; several person-related factors that can bias assessments; ways to select, administer, and use assessments in counseling; and ethical considerations.

The other relevant core area is Research and Program Evaluation. This includes basic methods of research, statistical techniques, and legal and ethical issues. Specifically mentioned are research designs, parametric and nonparametric statistics, needs assessment, and computer management and analysis of data.

State Certification Standards

A 1993 survey of state licensing requirements in school counseling conducted by the Educational TestingService is described by Ekstrom, Elmore and Schafer (in press). Courses in measurement, evaluation, and assessment are required in 29 states. Courses in assessing and interpreting aptitudes, interests, and achievements are required in 19 states. Eleven states require coursework in appraisal and evaluation, while two require psychological testing and measurement courses, two require testing and evaluation courses, one requires an academic and human assessment course, and one requires a course in analyzing verbal and non-verbal behavior.

Courses in program evaluation are mandated by 36 states

and 30 states have requirements for coursework in research methods. Such coursework typically includes statistical techniques that support both research and assessment.

Needed Assessment Competencies

Ongoing work by a committee of the American School Counselor Association and the Association for Assessment in Counseling has resulted in evolving drafts of a statement of standards for school counselors in the area of assessment and evaluation. Although neither finalized nor approved, some of these drafts have been discussed in workshop and panel presentations at conferences. Our recommendations are guided by that work.

Assessments come in many varieties. There are highly formal strategies, such as tests and surveys, informal approaches, such as observations and interviews, and a range of techniques in between, such as performance assessments and checklists. Each has advantages and disadvantages. The school counselor should know how to evaluate these for local use, including where to find the needed information for the evaluation and what sort of information each assessment type yields.

Nationally, certain assessment instruments are more commonly used than others in schools. We can all think of specific examples used to measure intelligence, achievements, interests, and abilities. The school counselor should know which tests are most common and how to evaluate them, including knowing where to look to obtain information and the dimensions instruments should be evaluated on.

School counselors often assist in administration of assessments. They should be able to implement procedures described in a manual, which may include computer administration, and understand why standardization is important. They should also be able to modify administration appropriately to accommodate special needs. As a leader in the school-based testing program, the school counselor should be able to provide information about administration (e.g., instructions about mechanics for teachers administering tests) and scoring (e.g., self-scoring for students on career exploration instruments) and know when it is necessary to obtain informed consent from parents or guardians before testing.

Whether for individuals or groups, reporting and interpreting assessments is typically part of the role of school counselors. Thus, they should understand and be able to explain how common scoring systems convey information about an assessment outcome (e.g., a percentile or other transformed score) and its degree of uncertainty (e.g., a transformed score band). They should be able to evaluate the appropriateness of norm groups for individual interpretations and their own ability to assess atypical students, which may necessitate appropriate consultation. They should also understand what rights and restrictions exist about disclosure and know how to use test information.

Ultimately, assessments exist because they are useful in decision making. The school counselor should be able to evaluate how well the available information supports decisions that are to be made, and should understand how information from multiple sources enhances the quality of decisions. Counselors must also be able to evaluate their own and others' limitations in using assessment results.

School counselors should be able to evaluate both long-term counseling programs and short-term interventions as part of their action research agendas. They should understand why and how evaluations are typically conducted. They should be able to consider whether the impacts, intended and unintended, of evaluation-based decisions are positive, and whether available information is adequate to justify decision making.

Some statistical expertise is necessary to engage in test and program evaluation activities. School counselors should be able to describe and interpret data from one variable (e.g., means, standard deviations, histograms) or two variables (e.g., correlation coefficients, scatter diagrams), relate a score to a normal distribution, use test-based data to evaluate a test (e.g., reliability and validity coefficients, standard errors of measurement), and evaluate whether statistical inferences are justified (e.g., hypothesis tests using chi-square, t, and F). Using computers to manage and process data would also enhance the repertoire of skills of the school counselor.

Not all local needs are satisfied by published instruments. Therefore, the school counselor should be able to implement assessment methods to meet specific needs. This includes procedures for specifying what an instrument should measure, formatting it, providing directions for its use, scoring it, and giving feedback.

Society is, by and large, illiterate about assessment (Stiggins, 1991). Thus, it falls to those who use assessments to ensure appropriate use. For the school counselor, an understanding of the nature of responsible assessment practice is essential. This includes familiarity with existing codes and standards as well as legal and ethical principles. It also entails obtaining credentials to document, and professional development to maintain currency of counseling skills.

Conclusion

Specific competencies like those mentioned could improve school counselors' assessment and evaluation activities. Also helpful would be links to counseling tasks and aids, such as self-tests for school counselors to use in evaluating their own abilities. Nevertheless, the progress that has been made toward standards is encouraging. These recommendations can be used even now by individual counselors and counselor educators in decision making. We encourage such use.

References

American Association of School Administrators, National Association of Elementary School Principals, National Association of Secondary School Principals, & National Council on Measurement in Education (AASA, NAESP, NASSP, & NCME). (1994). Competency standards in student assessment for educational administrators. *Educational Measurement: Issues and Practice, 13*(1), 44-47.

American Federation of Teachers, National Council on Measurement in Education, & National Education Association (AFT, NCME, & NEA). (1990). Standards for teacher competence in educational assessment of students. *Educational Measurement: Issues and Practice, 9*(4), 30-32.

Council for Accreditation of Counseling and Related Educational Programs (CACREP). (1994). *CACREP accreditation standards and procedures manual.* Alexandria, VA: Author.

Ekstrom, R B., Elmore, P. B., & Schafer. W. D. (in press). Standards for educational and psychological tests and testing professionals. In R. F. Dillon (Ed.), *Handbook on testing.* Westport, CT: Greenwood Publishing Group.

Impara, J. C. (1995). *Assessment skills of counselors, principals, and teachers.* Greensboro, NC: Counseling and Student Services Clearinghouse. (ERIC Document Reproduction Service No. EDO-CG-95-1).

Schafer, W. D. (1995). *Assessment skills for school counselors.* Greensboro, NC: Counseling and Student Services Clearinghouse. (ERIC Document Reproduction Service No. EDO-CG-95-2).

Schafer, W. D., & Lissitz, R. W. (1987). Measurement training for school personnel: Recommendations and reality. *Journal of Teacher Education, 38*(3), 57-63.

Stiggins, R. J. (1991). Assessment literacy. *Phi Delta Kappan, 72,* 534-539.

William D. Schafer is Associate Professor in the Department of Measurement, Statistics, and Evaluation at the University of Maryland, College Park.

Barbara Webster is a Professional School Counselor with the Edmond Public Schools, Edmond, Oklahoma.

27

The Politics of School Counseling

Jackie M. Allen

Overview

The profile of the 1990s is power politics. Groups with political clout are acknowledged and their issues are heard and acted upon. In contrast, groups lacking knowledge about or capability to use the political system, are unknown and their issues are not heard. As part of a very large educational system, school counselors can easily become lost in the enormous mutiplicity of issues, special programs, and specialists whose voices are heard by politicians— a system in which counselor issues are rarely heard and seldom understood.

The concept of "politics of school counseling" has grown out of a need for school counselors to be trained in survival skills to support the continuation of counseling and guidance programs coordinated by school counselors and to insure the ongoing existence of the profession. The traditional curriculum in school counselor training programs has had a heavy emphasis on counseling theory and technique, human growth and development, the organization and development of counseling programs, ethics, legal issues, assessment, and socio-cultural influences. Counseling specialities pertinent to school counselors have been developed in career counseling, family counseling, group counseling, and multicultural counseling.

In order for the school counselor to be successful on the job in the 1990s another group of practical skills, political skills, must be learned and become part of the school counselor's professional repertoire. These skills include advocacy and accountability, negotiation, facilitation of change, collaboration and coalition building, and fund raising and development. These political skills address the relevant needs of contemporary school counseling and, when learned, will prepare the school counselor for the demanding world of work in the public or private school system. Learning these new skills will empower the school counselor to save a counseling job, provide expanded services for students, and secure a future for the profession.

Advocacy and Accountability

Advocacy is a proactive expression of the value of counseling programs in terms of student outcomes. Advocacy takes many forms: school board presentations, letters to Congress, newspaper articles, video tapes, communications to parents, speeches to civic groups, program booklets, career days, and a variety of special activities.

School counselors are accountable to a variety of publics in the school and community. School counselor publics, such as the local school board, want to know what school counselors are doing and want to know what results are being produced. School boards, superintendents, local, county, and state departments of education, legislators, employers, parents, and students are questioning the cost effectiveness of school counseling programs and want to know if a counseling program really makes a measurable difference in student academic performance, school adjustment, readiness to learn, and preparation for the world of work.

Advocacy for school counseling is built on the solid foundation of accountability. School counselors need to know how to do action research. Accountability instruments assist school counselors in measuring their success. Such instruments must be chosen carefully and tailored to the desired data and the specific public to which the advocacy will be addressed. Client publics, educational system publics, and community publics look for appropriate accountability data which will demonstrate school counselor effectiveness in terms of student outcomes.

When making an advocacy presentation, school counselors must choose appropriate accountability instruments, plan to gather pertinent accountability data, know the interests of the specific public, and carefully select the method of presentation. Advocacy and accountability are vital tools for the school counselor to use in supporting, expanding, or improving the school counseling program.

Negotiation

Negotiation is not only for labor relations experts, sales people, or diplomats; negotiation skills are a powerful asset to all professionals. School counselors negotiate daily with teachers, administrators, parents, and students to improve their counseling programs. School counselors may use negotiation strategies and techniques to purchase new counseling and guidance curriculum materials or software, work out a date on the school calendar for a counseling and guidance function, secure funding for expanding the counseling and guidance program, modify evaluation criteria, obtain consensus of opinion on a student survey, agree on a change of working conditions or ratios with the union, or set realistic deadlines for a project.

Negotiation refers to the meeting of two or more individuals to discuss an idea or a concept with the intent of reaching an agreement. One individual may have what another individual wants, and bargaining will take place until the two individuals are satisfied with the deal or the agreement. At first, disagreement and conflict may threaten a resolution; but school counselors, already experienced in conflict resolution, will find that negotiation is an easy skill to acquire. School counselors also understand body language, communication skills, and personality factors which are essential elements for successful negotiation.

Current literature on negotiation emphases the "win-win" approach. The goal of compromise will assure a win-win situation. Knowing the ground rules, understanding what the other side wants, and working for a compromise will promote a satisfactory resolution for both parties. Becoming a good negotiator requires learning and practicing specific skills, knowledge of the principles that affect negotiating, and working toward the goal of mutual satisfaction. A capable negotiator must define goals and objectives, be able to clarify the issues, gather the pertinent background information, establish a rapport with the other side, and strive to settle the conflict with a resolution of the issues and an agreement that is a win-win situation for both parties.

School counselors becoming successful negotiators will enhance their abilities to improve counseling and guidance programs, mediate faculty-student disputes, deal more effectively with administrators, assist students to utilize the education system in planning for their future, and bring about change in the school system.

Facilitation of Change

Central to educational reform is change. The role of the school counselor in educational reform is that of a change agent. As change agent, the school counselor is a student advocate, catalyst, liaison to parents, systems thinker, provider of student services, transition consultant, policy-making facilitator, coordinator, team player, case manager, and leader in educational reform.

New skills are needed to prepare the school counselor to be a change agent. Change is facilitated by elastic thinking, flexible bodies, and the willingness to RISK by taking that quantum leap into the unknown where new philosophies, new structures, and new models are developed. In the literature, paradigm shift models applicable to school counseling are available in Stephen Covey's *Principle-Centered Leadership*, Joel Barker's *Future Edge*, and Burgess and Dedmond's *Quality Leadership and the Professional School Counselor*. The school counselor facilitates systemic change by being a part of and/or leading community councils, cooperative learning groups, strategic planning efforts, shared decision-making teams, advisory committees, or school improvement teams. The school counselor, as change agent, takes on an expanded role of not only coordinating a school-based comprehensive developmental guidance and counseling program but also coordinating community-based integrated counseling services, and coordinating school-to-work transition programs. The school counselor becomes the coordinator of individualized counseling and guidance services for students and a vital link between the educational system and business and industry.

Collaboration and Coalition Building

With increasing demands on school counselor time and energy, collaborative efforts are a necessity to provide the quality of counseling and guidance programs needed by today's young people. Learning to collaborate takes an open mind, a willingness to compromise, sharing a common mission, a knowledge of organizational structure and culture, an ability to work within a group, and a cooperative leadership style.

The school counselor is the most appropriate educator to facilitate "a culture of collaboration" in the local school community. The school counselor develops and nurtures collaborative relationships by facilitating change through programs of prevention and intervention for all students. Developing a culture of collaboration at the local school will unite students, faculty, staff, and the community in a common vision and mission to prepare each student to be successful in school and to acquire the essential skills for successful employment, responsible citizenship, and lifelong learning.

Many opportunities for collaboration are available starting at the local school site and reaching out into the community with school-to-work linkages to business and industry. Integrated services models such as the one developed through the Education Development Center project on "Integrating Pupil Services Personnel into Comprehensive School Health and HIV Prevention" promote comprehensive health education reform. Business partnerships provide professional expertise and technology for schools. Coalitions of pupil personnel organizations such as the National Association of Pupil Service Organizations (NAPSO) provide national leadership and support for legislative efforts. Through the collaboration of national organizations like the National Association for School Psychologists (NASP), the National Association of Social Workers (NASW), the American Counseling Association (ACA), and the American School Counselor Association (ASCA), a coalition was formed to pass the Elementary Counseling Demonstration Act.

Fund Raising and Development

The schools, as institutions created to fill a public need, are experiencing a decrease in funds each year as taxes are reduced or diverted to other public concerns. Due to the lack of funds many school districts are making fiscal decisions to reduce or cut school counseling programs and services. School counselors are faced with providing the same services with less resources and often less personnel. In order to survive, the school counselor must be able to locate funding and support for both intervention and prevention programs.

One of the new skill areas for school counselors is fund raising and development. A development officer seeks funding for an organization to carry out its mission and strategic plan. The school counselor of the future will need skills in grant writing. Grant writers need to be able to build consensus, formulate goals, strategically plan for multi-year projects, formulate budgets, be aware of the current issues, terminology, and politically appropriate trends, and articulate these programatic proposals in a timely manner. State and federal grant programs often have a short lead time and have very specific guidelines which must be followed in order to qualify for grant monies. Other sources for financial support include private foundations, business and industry, service organizations, community resources, and specially funded projects.

Conclusion

In order to meet the challenges of the present and be prepared for the future, school counselors must acquire a new set of skills which will enable them to promote and support successfully current programs, renew the profession, and envision a new future. The first step to empowerment is the acquisition of a set of self-help skills which will serve the school counselor in shaping his/her destiny. The power techniques of the 1990s: advocacy and accountability, facilitation of change, collaboration and coalition building, and fund raising and development can transform school counselors into politically astute professionals who are heard, understood, recognized, and supported for their importance in promoting student success.

References

Allen, J. (1994). *School counselors collaborating for student success*. Greensboro, NC: ERIC/CASS (EDO-CG-94-27).

Allen, J., & Gallagher, J. (1994). *Accountability for counselor advocacy*. An American School Counselor Association pamphlet.

Dawson, R. (1994). *Power negotiating workshop*. Niles, IL: Nightingale Conant Corporation.

Maddux, R. B. (1988). *Successful negotiation* (rev. ed.). Los Altos, CA: Crisp Publications.

Scott, C. P., & Jaffe, D. T. (1989). *Managing organizational change: A practical guide for managers*. Los Altos, CA: Crisp Publications.

Jackie M. Allen, Ed. D., NCC, NCSC, MFCC is on the faculty of Chapman University and is a consultant with Allen Consulting Associates.

28

School Counseling as a Specialty Area of the Profession

Pamela O. Paisley & L. DiAnne Borders

Overview

School counseling as a specialty area emerged—and continues to evolve—as a result of social, educational, political, and economic trends. Specifically, at the beginning of the twentieth century, divergent needs of public school populations required the inclusion of specialized assistance for students beyond that which was commonly and previously offered by teachers. The need for such specialized assistance for students remains apparent today.

The first school guidance programs appeared in the late 1800s and were closely connected to vocational education. Early programs were directive in nature and involved the provision of guidance classes to promote character development, teach socially appropriate behaviors, and assist with vocational planning. Reviews of the historical development of this specialty indicate that the scope and focus of school counseling programs changed over time: from vocational and educational decision-making, to personal growth, to responsive services for special "at-risk" populations, to developmental programs available for all students.

The focus has changed in response to a number of factors. While some of these influences were significant for the entire counseling profession (e.g., the Industrial Revolution, placement efforts by the military, the work of individuals such as Frank Parsons and Carl Rogers), other factors have had a more direct impact on the evolution of *school* counseling.

This digest is an abbreviated version of an article published in the *Journal of Counseling and Development* (Paisley & Borders), 1995. This abbreviated version is reprinted with the permission of the American Counseling Association. Please refer to the original article for a more extensive reference and resource list and a more detailed discussion of the content.

Influence of Federal Legislation

Federal legislation has been particularly significant in the creation and definition of counseling positions in public schools. The National Defense Education Act (1958), and the Elementary and Secondary Education Act (1965) provided particular opportunities for training school counselors and implementing specialized programs. Depending on the focus of the legislation, these programs provided services for vocationally oriented and college-bound students, school dropouts, and economically and academically disadvantaged young people. Legislation continues to influence the focus of this specialty area as most recently evident in the potential effects of the School-to-Work Opportunities Act (1994) and the Elementary School Counseling Demonstration Act (1994).

Influence of Professional Associations

The creation of a professional association specifically for school counselors also contributed greatly to the development of the specialty. Although not one of the founding divisions of the American Personnel and Guidance Association (APGA), the American School Counseling Association (ASCA) became the fifth division in 1953. Through discussion, debate, and publication of role statements, position papers, and ethical standards, this division has been very influential in the direction and shape of school counseling as it is known today.

The Association for Counselor Education and Supervision (ACES) and the National Career Development Association (NCDA) have also had a special interest in this area. ACES has sponsored program sessions, special roundtable discussions, an interest network, and collaborative efforts related to school counseling. NCDA members have supported federal legislation focused on school-to-work transition and have helped maintain a focus on school counselor involvement in career education, development, and planning for students.

In the past fifteen years, several specific projects have been sponsored by these professional associations to consider the future of this specialty area and to address school counseling concerns. Examples of these special efforts can be seen in
    (a) specific position statements adopted by ASCA,
    (b) "think tanks" supported by ACA,
    (c) ACES School Counseling Interest Networks at the

regional and national level,

(d) the ACES Roundtable on School Counseling Preparation Programs,

(e) the 20/20 Conference co-sponsored by ACA and the Educational Resources Information Center/Counseling and Personnel Services Clearinghouse (ERIC/CAPS), and

(f) establishment of an AACD School Counseling Task Force (1987).

Discussion

From these types of efforts, as well as from continued dialogue and discussion among school counselors, counselor educators, and counselor supervisors, a reconceptualization of the specialty area has occurred. Currently, the appropriate focus for school counseling is considered to be on comprehensive, developmental, and collaborative programs. Such programs include individual, small group, and large group counseling as well as consultation and coordination. These programs still offer certain types of responsive services related to remediation and crisis intervention, but they now emphasize primary prevention, promotion of healthy development for *all* students, and collaboration with other adults in the school, community, and family. Descriptions of, and rationale for, such developmental programs are readily available in the professional literature (e.g., ASCA position and role statements; Gysbers & Henderson, 1994; Myrick, 1993; Paisley & Hubbard, 1994).

Specialty Training Standards, Accreditation, and Certification

School counseling graduate training programs are affected by the standards of several accrediting bodies including the Council for the Accreditation of Counseling and Related Educational Programs (CACREP), the National Council for Accreditation of Teacher Education (NCATE), various state departments of education, and university graduate schools. The most rigorous of those standards are from the accrediting body most closely aligned with the profession: CACREP. These standards require that school counseling students have certain core counseling courses as well as specialty courses and practica.

School counselors also have access to several levels of certification and/or licensure. Each state has specific requirements for counselor certification which, while varying greatly, tend to be based on coursework, practica, and, sometimes, teaching experience. National certification is also available through the National Board of Certified Counselors (NBCC). Nationally Certified School Counselors (NCSC) are required to first meet the generic requirements to become a Nationally Certified Counselor (NCC), and then must complete specialty requirements related to school counseling. Many school counselors who have completed necessary course work and supervision also choose to become Licensed Professional Counselors (LPC) within their states.

When taken as a whole, national specialty training standards, accreditation, and certification provide a significant professional statement. They recognize the specialty area's rights and responsibilities to define the scope of school counseling programs and the role of school counseling practice.

Future Issues and Trends

The future of school counseling will be greatly impacted by the nature of and changes within society, which will affect students, families, and schools. Demographic information describes a context for children and adolescents which includes divorce, poverty, violence, and neglect. School counselors will increasingly face issues associated with single-parent and blended families, greater use of technology, and the diverse nature of the culture in which we live. Relevant changes in the counseling program and the counselor's workday will be necessary.

Discussions of the future of this specialty will also require ongoing examination of the school counselor's role and evaluation of program effectiveness. Currently, a school counselor's role continues to be either explicitly or implicitly defined by a number of sources, few of whom have any background or experience in school counseling and who often provide somewhat contradictory direction. Additionally, the counselor role is affected by state and federal legislation about—and funding for—the provision of counseling services in the school. Such legislation often has positive effects, such as those previously noted as related to the National Defense Education Act. Some legislation, however, has adverse effects, sometimes negatively redefining the school counselor's job. These adverse effects can be seen in legislation that encourages the use of part time—and sometimes unqualified—employees for specialized counseling work (e.g., drop-out prevention, substance abuse) or that includes funding specifications with such narrow definitions (e.g., financial brackets, personal characteristics) of who may be served that some students are "ineligible" to receive the services they need.

Relatedly, it seems that educational administrators, legislators, school reformers, and others think almost exclusively of teachers when making decisions about schools. It often appears that school counselors are overlooked by these persons; at best, counselors are misunderstood. To be viable contributors in school-based decision-making and reform efforts, school counselors and counselor educators and supervisors will have to be assertive in their attempts to become involved at both the national and local level.

Discussion of the counselor's role will also need to include evaluation of program and intervention effectiveness. This evaluation will assist in determining the best use of counselor time and the most appropriate focus for interventions. Continued consideration and evaluation of the application of particular models (e.g., brief therapy and family therapy models) in schools will be especially helpful.

Additionally, regardless of how counseling is defined, the complexity of the role is such that ongoing supervision for school counselors will be critical. There is ample evidence that such supervision is not currently being provided in the schools and that it is a high priority for practitioners (Roberts & Borders, 1994). Innovative programs will be needed to address this area of continued professional development.

Conclusion

As school counseling moves forward into the twenty-first century, educators and practitioners would do well to remember the history and evolutionary nature of the specialty. It is unlikely that the dialogue or debate concerning school counseling is complete. The discussion will continue to be a dynamic one as the needs of children and adolescents change and as we understand more about the most effective interventions. As we continue to participate in this evolution, the recommendations of a recent ASCA president provide significant guidance: that school counselors become *catalysts* for change, who are proactive rather than reactive, *communicators* advocating for themselves, *caregivers* for self and others, and *collaborators* in providing the best and most appropriate services for children and adolesents (Allen, 1993).

References

Allen, J. M. (1993). The professional school counselor: Decision-making facilitator and agent of change. *Education career directory* (1st ed.), pp. 61 - 65. Detroit, MI: Visible Ink Press.

Gysbers, N. C., & Henderson, P. (1994). *Developing and managing your school guidance program.* Alexandria, VA: American Counseling Association.

Myrick, R. D. (1993). *Developmental guidance and counseling: A practical approach* (2nd ed.). Minneapolis, MN: Educational Media Corporation.

Paisley, P. O., & Borders, L. D. (1995). School counseling: An evolving specialty. *Journal of Counseling and Development, 74,* 150 - 513.

Paisley, P. O., & Hubbard, G. T. (1994). *Developmental school counseling programs: From theory to practice.* Alexandria, VA: American Counseling Association.

Roberts, E. B., & Borders, L. D. (1994). Supervision of school counselors: Administrative, program, and counseling. *The School Counselor, 41* (3), 149 - 157.

Pamela Paisley is an Associate Professor and School Counseling Program Coordinator in the Department of Counseling and Human Development Services at The University of Georgia in Athens.

L. DiAnne Borders is a Professor of Counselor Education and Department Chair at The University of North Carolina at Greensboro.

29

The Internet as a Resource for School Counseling

Ellen B. Rust

Overview

Since February 1993, counselors around the world have been sharing ideas over the Internet. Dozens of counselors have participated in discussions on timely issues and have responded to requests for information or resources. The International Counselor Network (ICN), an electronic mail (email) discussion group operating on the Internet, has provided these, and many other, opportunities. As counselor use of the Internet has grown, the need for further services has become apparent. Recent initiatives have started what will soon become a commonplace and necessary resource for school counselors: counselor-specific information databases on the Internet. This chapter describes the counseling resources that presently exist and proposes the development of more.

Development of Internet

The Internet began as a U.S. Department of Defense experiment over 20 years ago. Today this global network connects 25 million people, with more "coming online" everyday. The number of host computers providing services on the Internet grew from 235 in May, 1982 to more than 3.2 million in July, 1994 (Pike, Kent, Husain, Kinnaman, & Menges, 1994). Online services provide electronic information of all kinds, including news, software, email, and reference materials. Many organizations have information on servers which can be searched easily. New information databases are being created daily, at a phenomenal rate.

The Internet is not just a network of computer networks, it is also the people who use it and the information contained on it (Krol & Hoffman, 1993). This network of networks "fosters an unparalleled degree of communication, collaboration, resource sharing, and information access" (Tennant, 1992). A technology writer who has been online for twenty years predicts that "by the year 2000, anyone in the civilized world will be able to get the answer on the Internet to any question whose answer is known or calculable" (Pournelle, 1995).

Although K-12 educators and the general public have just recently discovered the resourcefulness of the Internet, researchers have been using it for years. Anyone can get regular information from news groups, also known as bulletin boards, and from email discussion lists. Email, the sending and receiving of messages electronically over telephone and computer networks that may be stored and read at the receiver's convenience, is a useful tool for communicating with colleagues and friends. Just as the radio, television, and telephone reduced the isolation of most of the world earlier in this century, the Internet can bring an unlimited amount of knowledge and information into every home, school, and business.

World Wide Web

An area of the Internet which has experienced almost exponential growth is the World Wide Web (WWW). A series of multimedia documents (text, images, sounds, movies) connected by hyperlinks, the WWW "enables users to click on words in a document to call forth other documents, link after link, from around the world" (Neubarth, 1995). In the Spring of 1995, the American School Counselor Association and the ERIC Clearinghouse on Counseling and Student Services collaborated to establish a "home page" for ASCA on the ERIC/CASS WWW site at the School of Education, University of North Carolina, Greensboro. This "home page" (hyperlinked document) now provides both a counselor-specific database, and links to other information servers. Information available here includes an overview of ASCA, a directory of current officers and committee chairs, ASCA publications and dates and locations of ASCA conferences. Two of the most useful links connect the user to the ERIC Digest server and to the AskERIC search program. Easy to understand guides explain how to conduct searches for information. ASCA's Information Technology Committee and the ERIC/CASS staff manage the selection and updating of material. This site may be reached by "pointing" your WWW browser to: http://www.uncg.edu/~ericcas2.

Gopher

Gopher is a menu-based information retrieval system for exploring the resources of the Internet. It was started at the

University of Minnesota (the "Golden Gophers") as a campus information service which would "go fer" things. There are now hundreds of Gopher servers on the Internet. The CounselorNet Gopher was established at the State University of New York, Plattsburgh in late fall, 1994 as a collaborative project of Tod Spedding, a graduate student at University of Alaska, Virginia Brady, a graduate of the Community Counseling program at SUNY/Plattsburgh, and Dr. Mary Roark, Professor at SUNY/Plattsburgh. The idea for CounselorNet originated with Tod, who contributed much of the content of the original Site Index. CounselorNet maintains an index to materials on the Internet useful for counselors in schools, agencies, and colleges and is available through the Gopher server at SUNY/Plattsburgh. It offers practical, user-friendly access to a wide array of resources on the Internet which are relevant to the work of a counselor. A unique feature of CounselorNet is its mentor program, whereby experienced counselors can provide educational information directly to others on the Internet. Access to this resource is via Gopher.Plattsburgh.edu 70. CounselorNet can also be reached via the World Wide Web at Gopher:// baryon.hawk.plattsburgh.edu 70.

International Counselor Network

The International Counselor Network (ICN) was founded by the author in the Winter of 1993 in order to cut down on the isolation felt by many counselors who do not have the time or opportunity to connect with colleagues in person. Since then, it has grown to more than 500 subscribers and is read in almost every one of the 50 states and the Canadian provinces. Counselors in Australia, Brazil, England, Finland, Germany, Malaysia, Spain, Taiwan, Thailand, and Turkey participate in the discussions as well. ICN members collaborate by sharing ideas, resources, and discourse about mental health issues and related technology applications. Topics have included self-esteem, multicultural issues, restructuring guidance programs, conflict resolution, career planning, play therapy, abuse, application of counseling theories, interactive multimedia, counselor training and assessment, and a comparison of counseling in different parts of the country or world.

One of the most useful features of the ICN is the ability to be instantly in touch with dozens of counselors around the world. An email request to the network can result in a reply within the next few hours, sometimes sooner. Counselor educators occasionally ask the counselors in the field for input when developing courses for their programs. Members share articles or papers they have written and ask for comments or reactions. News about upcoming workshops, conferences, and legislation is posted. Those who are more familiar with the Internet guide newcomers to useful areas.

In order to join the International Counselor Network, send an email message to listserv@utkvm1.utk.edu and in the body of the mail message, write: subscribe icn <your first name> <your lastname>. For example, I would write: *subscribe icn ellen rust*.

Other Resources

The ICN is only one of many avenues for communication, information sharing, and collaboration. Similar listservs are being established to announce current and upcoming developments, and to meet the needs of other divisions within the American Counseling Association. CESNET-L, a listserv for Counselor Educators and Supervisors, was started in the fall of 1994 by Marty Jencius, a graduate student at the University of South Carolina, with the encouragement of several ACES members. CATS2, the Counselor and Therapist Support System, began in the Spring of 1995. Initiated by ERIC/CASS, this moderated interprofessional listserv focuses on critical topics for counselors and therapists. SCIF, the School Counseling Issues Forum, was planned to begin in the Fall, 1995 under the sponsorship of ASCA. Many other listservs of interest to counselors are listed in a document on the ASCA home page.

Conclusion

As more counselors take advantage of information technology, additional databases should be started to meet the needs. Sessions to train counselors to use these new resources need to be held at state, regional, and national conferences.

The new information technologies are already shaping the way business is conducted. Educators are already retooling for the 21st–century needs of critical thinking and team problem solving. Counselors have the skills and training to assist students and staff in the restructuring of the school climate and the learning environment. We are uniquely positioned to be facilitators of change (Perry, 1992). Participating in the new technologies will give us the advantage.

The International Counselor Network has provided a forum for discussion and new ideas. The discussion groups and databases mentioned above can expand the expertise of counselors in both rural and urban areas. It is time for school counselors to get on the cutting edge of the information revolution.

References

Krol, E., & Hoffman, E. (1993). FYI on "What Is the Internet?" *Information About the Internet.* Nashville, TN: South Central Bell.

Neubarth, M. (1995, April). "Web fever: Catch it!" *Internet World,* p. 4.

Perry, N.S. (1992). Educational reform and the school counselor. Ann Arbor, MI: ERIC Clearinghouse on Counseling and Personnel Services. (ERIC Digest ED347491)

Pike, M.A., Kent, P., Husain, K., Kinnaman, D., & Menges, D. C. (1994). *Using Mosaic* (p. 15). Indianapolis: Que Corporation.

Pournelle, J. (1995, March). "Civilization, free expression, and the net." *Internet World,* p. 83.

Tennant, R. (1992). Internet basics. Syracuse, NY: ERIC Clearinghouse on Information Resources.(ERIC Digest ED348054)

Ellen B. Rust, MA, MEd, is a school counselor in the Metropolitan Nashville Public Schools.

Assessment for Advocacy and Accountability in School Counseling

Jan Gallagher

Overview

In today's educational community, there are key phrases such as "measures of assessment," " standards of accountability," "evaluation models" and "performance objectives," which many times are interchangeable and are sometimes redundant. The many education publics are very desirious of demonstrable outcomes that are clearly supported by research.

School counselors have been taught and admonished to keep good records. Because of the type and amounts of information kept for records, much data is accumulated; yet seldom is this data in the appropriate format for assessment, advocacy, or accountability. Counselors, because of their penchant for keeping good records, combined with the accessibility of computer technology, have all the ingredients for excellent documentation, reliable research, and proven success. What counselors must learn is how to ask the right questions, assimilate the necessary data (via computer for ease of management and implementation), and develop a report which creates a clear picture and presents a sound statement.

Let us begin by looking at some simple definitions:

Assessment - an appraisal or evaluation, analyzing critically and judging definitively the nature, significance, status, merits, or importance.

Advocacy - the action of advocating, pleading for, or supporting.

Accountability - the quality or state of being accountable, liable, or responsible, furnishing a justifying analysis or a detailed explanation.

Souces of Data Available to School Counselors

School counselors are often so caught up in dealing with a myriad of students and their problems, along with various other duties, that they fail to recognize the vast amounts and various kinds of data readily available, which can critically analyze our job responsibilities (assessment), prove the value of programs (advocacy) or measure the quality of performance as individuals or programs (accountability). Some sources of data are:

SURVEYS are data collection tools which solicit answers to questions from participants. A survey can pose questions or take measurements. Surveys may be done with parents, students, school staff, and community members. They may be school-oriented or for the use of the professional association. Surveys are classified by the method of gathering information: personal interview, telephone interview, mail questionnaire, panel, or a combination of methods.

QUALITATIVE QUESTIONNAIRES are used to measure a participant's opinion after an activity or intervention, such as a series of group counseling sessions. Qualitative research seeks to obtain information about the quality of a program or service. Questionnaires vary in length and format and may include open-ended questions.

CASE STUDIES constitute a brief description of a particular counseling case, interventions used, and results obtained. It is important to maintain the confidentiality of student names and particular details which might identify the student. Case studies help school counselors improve their counseling techniques and they serve as examples of school counselor effectiveness.

BEHAVIORAL OBSERVATIONS are planned in advance and usually refer behaviors that can be observed and are recorded. *INFORMAL* observations may consist of a running account of what a particular student is doing in a class. *FORMAL* behavioral observations may be made by using a checklist and looking for particular behaviors which will qualify a student for a special program.

NEEDS ASSESSMENTS are conducted to determine specific needs, in terms of school counseling programs and services.

SELF-AUDIT is a specialized needs assessment where an
audit is used as a self-appraisal instrument to determine
strengths and weaknesses. The American School
Counselor Association has prepared three self-audits
(available at ASCA Headquarters) for elementary, middle,
and secondary school levels.

EXPERIMENTAL (QUANTITATIVE) research designs include
many variations of pre-test and post-test assessments
where a cause or independent variable is present in the
study. This type of research is used effectively to measure
change as a result of counseling in areas such as classroom
behavioral interventions, small group interventions, and
individual counseling interventions.

ACCOUNTABILITY DATA comes from many sources such
as school counselor logs, conference record forms,
appointment sheets, student profile forms, grades,
behavior, and attendance records.

BIOGRAPHICAL OR PORTFOLIO DATA may be collected
during an interview, from a written form, or from student
work samples. School counselors use this type of data to
write college and scholarship recommendations.

Uses of Data by School Counselors

What kinds of data should be used? This is probably the first
question which comes to mind. A better idea is to start with the
question you are trying to answer. For example, if you wish to know
if counselors are seeing children, one could look at the sign-in log
and find this pertinent data. But what one really might want to
know is how does a counselor spend his/her time? How much of
that time is spent with children? Individually, in small groups, or in
classes? This might be accomplished with a time/task log kept by
the counselor over a period of time and then by compiling total
percentages of time spent in various categories of activities.

Another question might arise, such as "Did the counseling
make a difference for those involved?" That question might best be
answered by personal interviews compiled into a narrative summary.
The use of video interviews often can be used to document the
effectiveness or success of a program. A video is a very memorable
report medium.

By preparing a case study, or several case studies on the same
topic, a comprehensive technique/method of counseling might
presented. In a narrative form, these could be the basis for a journal

article or the beginning of a book.

Short, but opened-ended, questions collected at the beginning or ending of a presentation, a program, or a series of activities can provide a extensive review of participants' likes and/or dislikes, changes in participant attitudes, and or behaviors.

The possibilities of data collection and applications are endless. Counselors need to only recognize the data sources and use the information to its maximum.

Conclusion

There is ample information in counseling offices just waiting to be put into a comprehensive format to demonstrate and document success(es). Assessment for advocacy and accountability is simply a matter of deciding on the question, assembling the available and plentiful data into an informational format, and using that evidence to demonstrate success, change, and responsible activities. Counselors must seize these opportunities to recognize good practices and to highlight successful programs through sound, research-driven practices.

Resources

Allen, J., & Gallagher, J.(1991). *Accountability in counseling.* Alexandria, VA: ASCA.

Kerlinger, F. N. (1986). *Foundations of behavioral research.* Chicago, Il: Holt, Rinehart and Winston, Inc.

Norisis, M. J. (1988). *SPSS/PC + Studentware. Princeton, NJ:* SPSS Inc.

Orenstein A., & Phillips, W.R.F. (1978). *Understanding social research: An introduction. New York, NY:* Allyn and Bacon, Inc.

Jan Gallagher is the coordinator of Guidance & Testing in the Harlandale Independent School District in San Antonio, Texas. She is currently serving as the Post-Secondary/Supervisor Vice President of the American School Counselor Association.

ERIC/CASS Virtual Libraries: Online Resources for Parents, Teachers, and Counselors

Garry R. Walz & Jeanne C. Bleuer

Overview

As the developer of the world's largest and most frequently used education database and a pioneering leader in offering an Internet-based question-answering service, ERIC, the Educational Resources Information Center, is ideally suited to take leadership in the development of online virtual libraries. The virtual libraries described in this paper provide users with immediate, well-organized access to the full-text of hundreds of useful articles and documents on topics of high interest not only to education and counseling professionals, but also to parents, students, and the general public.

What is ERIC?

ERIC is a federally-funded program which was inaugurated in 1966 to serve as the nation's archive of important education documents. Over the years, the role of ERIC has expanded to incorporate not only the collection and storage of educational information, but also the generation of new information through publications and newsletters, the dissemination of information through question-answering services, and the provision of training in the use of information through workshops and conference presentations.

ERIC currently consists of a network of 16 subject-specific clearinghouses, 10 adjunct clearinghouses, and 4 supporting service components. It is sponsored by the U.S. Department of Education, Office of Educational Research and Improvement and administered by the National Library of Education.

What resources does ERIC offer?

- Access to "fugitive" documents such as research reports, curriculum guides, conference papers, etc., through *Resources in Education (RIE)* and the ERIC microfiche collection.
- Access to citations and annotations of articles from more than 900 education-related journals through the *Current Index to Journals in Education.*
- Question-answering services via toll-free phone numbers, fax, mail, e-mail, and in-person visits to clearinghouses and professional conference exhibits.
- Skill-building workshops on topics of high critical need and interest.
- Scope-specific publications that meet the information needs of each clearinghouse's audience.
- Opportunities for education professionals as well as parents and the general public to share their ideas, products, and research with one another through submission of documents to the ERIC database and/or participation in listservs.

How accessible are ERIC resources?

- The ERIC database is available in print, online, and CD-ROM versions.
- ERIC searching products and services are offered by four private online database vendors and five CD-ROM vendors.
- ERIC can be searched on the Internet at several ERIC Web sites.
- Access to ERIC microfiche and publications is provided by more than 1,000 institutions in 27 countries.
- An electronic question-answering service is provided by AskERIC.
- ERIC Web sites provide up-to-date information on ERIC and ERIC Clearinghouse services and activities.

What is ERIC/CASS?

One of the original ERIC Clearinghouses established in 1966, ERIC/CASS is the ERIC Clearinghouse that serves counseling and student services professionals as well as parents and others who have an interest in personal and social factors that affect learning and development. Examples of topics addressed by ERIC/CASS include: drugs, self-efficacy, conflict resolution, abuse, equity, life/career planning, and family functioning.

What are the ERIC/CASS Virtual Libraries?

During the past two years, the ERIC Clearinghouse on Counseling and Student Services (ERIC/CASS) at the University of North Carolina at Greensboro (UNCG) has undertaken a special initiative to develop several online virtual libraries. Each virtual library is designed to provide users with online access to an extensive array of full-text documents on a topic of current high interest and/or critical concern.

Advantages of a Virtual Library
- Ease of accessibility
- Low cost
- As intensive or extensive as desired
- Easy to update and expand
- Minimal hassle due to loss or non-return of borrowed items

Disadvantages of a Virtual Library
- Sometimes not as accessible or portable as libraries composed of "dead tree" (paper copy) items
- Potentially intimidating to "non-techy" types
- Can leave people feeling bereft at the lack of the feel and heft of a real book
- May appear to be difficult to scan for general impressions or skim for specific items
- Under the mantle of the Internet, may acquire an unwarranted reputation for objectivity and accuracy

The ERIC/CASS - NOICC Virtual Library of Career Development Resources

The first virtual library developed by ERIC/CASS was sponsored and funded by the National Occupational Information Coordinating Committee (NOICC) through a grant from its Career Development Training Institute (CDTI) program. With valuable input from NOICC's Executive Director, Dr. Juliette Lester, and the North Carolina State Occupational Information Coordinating Committee Director, Nancy MacCormac, ERIC/CASS staff collected, reviewed, scanned, and converted to HTML hundreds of useful ERIC documents, ERIC Digests, NOICC publications, and other non-copyrighted materials.

In addition to the input of existing materials, ERIC/CASS' Virtual Library Webmaster, Rob Bohall, developed numerous links to other relevant Websites, and ERIC/CASS Director, Dr. Garry Walz, developed a set of frequently asked questions and answers of special interest to parents.

To make the library easy to search, documents are cross-referenced and can be accessed through four categories: Subject Area, Population, Resources for Parents, and NOICC Resources. In addition to the full-text of several items in each area, an annotated bibliography of other relevant resources is provided.

ERIC/CASS Virtual Libraries: New for 1997

Based on the success and positive feedback on the ERIC/CASS-NOICC Virtual Library of Career Development Resources, ERIC/CASS, through special project funding from ERIC, developed five more virtual libraries during the first six months of 1997. They are:

(1). Learning and Achievement
(2). Substance Abuse
(3). School Violence
(4). School-to-Work Transition
(5). Multiculturalism, Diversity and Pluralism

These five new libraries were modeled after the career development library in that they provide user-friendly cross-references to documents, links to other relevant Websites, and annotated bibliographies of additional resources. Lists of the specific topics covered in all six virtual libraries is provided in Appendix A, and a summary of URLs to access each of the libraries is provided in Appendix B.

Coming in '98

ERIC/CASS is currently collecting and organizing resources for six more virtual libraries to be ready for public access by June of 1998. They include:

(1). Conflict Resolution
(2). Depression and Suicide
(3). Gangs
(4). Bullying
(5). Juvenile Boot Camps
(6). Assessment in Counseling and Therapy

Appendix A
Virtual Library Categories

Career Development Virtual Library
http://www.uncg.edu/~ericcas2/career/

Subject Areas
- Computerized Guidance & Information
- School-To-Work Transition
- Assessment and Portfolios
- One-Stop Career Centers
- Comprehensive Career Development
- Career Counseling Interventions
- Program Evaluation
- Labor Market Trends and Info
- Staff Development and Training

Job Search Sites
- America's Job Bank
- America's Talent Bank
- Canada Work Network
- Career Magazine
- Career Path
- E-Span
- JobBank USA
- JOBTRAK
- The Monster Board
- Online Career Center

NOICC Resources
- Links to SOICC's
- Nat'l Career Development Guidelines
- NOICC Occasional Papers
- Products and Services

Specific Populations
- Adults
- College Students
- Ethnic Groups
- K-12 Students
- Non-Employed
- Out-of-School Youths
- Persons with Disabilities
- Women

Resources for Parents
- Career Exploration & Decision-Making
- College Selection & Financial Aid
- Employment Bound Youth
- Employability Skills
- FrequentlyAsked Questions
- Job-Seeking Skills
- Related Organizations
- Training Options
- Work-Based Learning

Reference Shelf
- Index of On-Site Documents
- Virtual Library FAQ's
- Index of On-Site ERIC Digests
- Lists of Links: Careers, Labor Market
- New Acquisitions
- User Survey
- Virtual Library FAQ's

Cultural Diversity Virtual Library
http://www.uncg.edu/~ericcas2/diverse/index.htm

Student Level
Early Childhood and Elementary
Secondary
Higher Education
Adult Education

Practitioner Role
Administrators
Counselors
Teachers

Resources for Parents
Family Influence on Students
Helping Plan for the Future
Parent/School Relationship

Ethnic Groups
Asian
Black
Hispanic
Native American

Special Needs Students
Gay/Lesbian
Limited English Proficient
Migrant Students
Students with Disabilities

Special Topics
Assessment
Bilingual Education and ESL
Discrimination in Education
Promising Programs

School-To-Work Transition Virtual Library
http://www.uncg.edu/~ericcas2/stw_tran/index.htm

Student Level
Elementary
Secondary
College/Postsecondary

Practitioner Role
Administrators
Counselors
Teachers

Special Topics
Career Development
Legislation and Policy
Performance Standards
Special Needs Students

Effective Programs
Creating & Evaluating
    Programs
Current Issues
Employers and STW

Resources for Parents
Family Influence
Parental Involvement
School-To-Work Basics

Substance Abuse in Education Virtual Library
http://www.uncg.edu/~ericcas2/substnce/index.htm

Student Level
- Elementary
- Secondary
- College/Postsecondary

Practitioner Role
- Administrators
- Counselors
- Teachers

Special Topics
- Peer Counseling
- Pre-Natal Exposure
- Promising Programs
- Rehabilitation

Specific Substances
- Alcohol
- Illegal Drugs
- Steroids
- Tobacco

Resources for Parents
- Communication
- Treatment
- Prevention
- Signs of Abuse

Student Learning and Achievement Virtual Library
http://www.uncg.edu/~ericcas2/achieve/

Student Level
- Elementary
- Secondary
- College/Postsecondary

Practitioner Role
- Administrators
- Counselors
- Teachers

Special Topics
- Student Motivation
- Alternative School Searches
- Career Planning

Special Needs Students
- Economically Disadvantaged
- Ethnic Minorities
- Gifted and Talented
- Students with Disabilities

Resources for Parents
- Specific Curriculum Areas
- Improving Academic Skills
- Family Impact
- Testing and Grades

School Violence Virtual Library
http://www.uncg.edu/~ericcas2/violence/index.htm

Student Level
    Elementary
    Secondary
    College/Postsecondary

School Safety
    Punishment and Intervention
    School Environment
    Security Measures
    Violence Policy

Special Topics
    Corporal Punishment
    Crisis Intervention
    Guns
    Media Impact

Practitioner Role
    Administrators
    Counselors
    Teachers

Resources for Parents
    Avoiding Violence
    Dealing with Violent Children
    Family Influence
    Parent/School Relationship

Appendix B
Virtual Library URL's

ERIC/CASS Virtual Libraries
http://www.uncg.edu/~ericcas2

- **Career Development**
  http://www.uncg.edu/edu/ericcass/career/index.htm

- **Cultural Diversity**
  http://www.uncg.edu/edu/ericcass/diverse/index.htm

- **School-To-Work Transition**
  http://www.uncg.edu/edu/ericcass/stw_tran/index.htm

- **School Violence**
  http://www.uncg.edu/edu/ericcass/violence/index.htm

- **Student Learning and Achievement**
  http://www.uncg.edu/edu/ericcass/achieve/index.html

- **Substance Abuse**
  http://www.uncg.edu/edu/ericcass/substnce/index.htm

About ERIC and ERIC/CASS

ERIC/CASS (originally ERIC/CAPS) was one of the original Clearinghouses which formed the Educational Resources Information Center (ERIC) in 1966. ERIC has since grown to be the world's largest educational data base with nearly one million entrees.

The ERIC system has as its mission to improve American education by increasing and facilitating the use of educational research and information on practice in the activities of learning, teaching, educational decision-making, and research, wherever and whenever these activities take place.

ERIC is made up of sixteen separate Clearinghouses, each of which has a specific focus. The ERIC Counseling & Student Services Clearinghouse (ERIC/CASS) has its major foci serving the needs and interests of care givers and helping specialists such as counselors, therapists, career specialists, etc., at all ages and educational levels and in all settings—school, college, government, business and private practice.

Our basic goal has been to improve decision making through increased access to information. More importantly, we strive through the many resources and services we offer, to empower our users to more fully realize their goals and —yes— their dreams as well!

NETWORK WITH ERIC/CASS!

On a regular basis ERIC/CASS disseminates information about important topics to members of special interest and professional focus networks. Among the items distributed are newsletters, announcements of new products and resources, ERIC Digests, new releases, workshop and conference information, and updates on new developments in ERIC and information technology. If you are interested in becoming an ERIC/CASS Networker, please complete this form.

Name: _____

Preferred Title: ☐Mr. ☐Mrs. ☐Ms. ☐Dr.

Address: _____

_____

City: _____ State: _____ Zip: _____

Phone Numbers:

Home: _____ Office: _____

FAX: _____

Internet Address : _____

Position: _____ Level/Setting: _____

_Counselor/Therapist   _ Elementary School   _ Community Agency
_School Psychologist   _ Middle/Junior High School   _ Government Agency
_Social Worker   _ High School   _ Professional
_Counselor Educator   _ K-12/District Office   Association
_School Psych. Educator   _ Intermediate School Dist.   _ Private Practice
_Social Work Educator   _ Junior/Community College   _ Other
_Administrator   _ College/University   _____
_Student
_Other

Major Interests:

1._____ 2._____ 3. _____

Mail To:
ERIC/CASS NETWORKER
201 Ferguson Building
University of North Carolina at Greensboro
PO Box 26171
Greensboro, NC 27402-6171
FAX (336) 334-4116

ERIC/CASS
Website

University of North Carolina at Greensboro
School of Education
201 Ferguson Building   UNCG
Greensboro, NC 27402-6171
http://www.uncg.edu/~ericcas2

One of the best sources of educational information is ERIC—the Educational Resources Information Center. An appropriate first step in gaining access to ERIC is to locate the ERIC/CASS Website and through it identify a multitude of educational resources. Numerous "hotlinks" to other databases and websites can also be reached through the ERIC/CASS Website.

Through ERIC/CASS, the U.S. Department of Education's extensive educational resources can be accessed as well as special services of the ERIC system (AskERIC, Access ERIC and other ERIC Clearinghouses). Among the specific resources available on the ERIC/CASS Website are:

- Search capability of the ERIC database through the U.S. Department of Education
- Information on forthcoming ERIC/CASS Listservs
- Full text ERIC/CASS Digests
- Information on forthcoming conferences and workshops
- Shopping mall of publications and resources

For more information on ERIC/CASS, call (336) 334-4114, FAX (336) 334-4116, e-mail: ericcas@hamlet.uncg.edu, or access the ERIC/CASS Homepage at:

http://www.uncg.edu/~ericcas2

Counseling Employment Bound Youth

Edwin L. Herr Ed.D.

At last, the monograph so many persons have needed and have sought for so long. Employment bound youth, a large and vital segment of our population (20 million plus) and future labor force, have been largely ignored in the literature on careers and on counseling and guidance.

This neglect has clearly been to the great detriment not only of the young people themselves, but to our country's vitality and competitiveness in the rapidly expanding global economy.

In seven vital chapters, Dr. Herr covers the topics which make this monograph both a thought piece and a practical handbook. The basic topics covered are:

- *Employment-bound youth: Diversity in characteristics, opportunities and support*
- *The emerging economic investment for employment-bound youth*
- *Career development for employment-bound youth in schools*
- *The school-to-work transition for the employment-bound youth*
- *Career counseling for employment-bound youth*
- *The counselor and related career interventions*
- *Epilogue—Challenges to and the future of career counseling and guidance*

1995 302 pages $19.95

A Visit to a Comprehensive Guidance Program That Works

**Northside
Independent
School District
San Antonio,Texas**

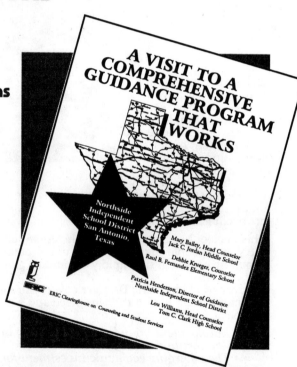

A detailed description of how a comprehensive school guidance program was implemented in an actual operating school setting. This volume addresses the issues and concerns of administrators and practitioners who make a program work.

1996   140 pages $17.50